SÃO [

GROWTH AND

POVERTY

C2 £299

⑧ M

Cândido Procópio Ferreira de Camargo

Fernando Henrique Cardoso

Frederico Mazzucchelli

José Álvaro Moisés

Lúcio Kowarick

Maria Hermínia Tavares de Almeida

Paul Israel Singer

Vinícius Caldeira Brant

SÃO PAULO GROWTH AND POVERTY

A report from the São Paulo
Justice and Peace Commission
Introduction by Cardinal Arns,
Archbishop of São Paulo

THE BOWERDEAN PRESS

in association with

THE CATHOLIC INSTITUTE FOR INTERNATIONAL RELATIONS

1978

First published in 1978 by The Bowerdean Press,
15 Blackfriars Lane, London EC4V 6ER
in association with The Catholic Institute
for International Relations, 1 Cambridge Terrace
Regents Park, London NW1 4JL

Designed by Douglas Martin
Printed in Great Britain by
A.B. Printers Ltd, Leicester

Photographic credits: Antonio Carlos D'Ávila,
Antonio José Saggese, Augusto Ramasco,
Carlos Alberto Ebert, Juca Martins,
Paulo Vasconcelos, Ruth Toledo, *Agência Estado*

British Library Cataloguing in Publication Data

Roman Catholic Church. *Archdiocese of São Paulo. Pontifícia Comissão de Justiça e Paz*
São Paulo Growth and Poverty.
1. São Paulo, Brazil (City) — Social conditions
2. São Paulo, Brazil (City) — Economic conditions
I. Title II. Catholic Institute for International Relations

ISBN 0 906097 02 9 (paperback)
ISBN 0 906097 01 0 (cased)

CONTENTS

Foreword

São Paulo is the fastest growing city in the world—from little more than a small town a hundred years ago to a huge sprawling metropolis with some 12 million people today. It currently ranks amongst the six largest cities in the world and will probably be the largest by the end of the century. If its current growth rate of 4.2% a year is maintained, the inhabitants of São Paulo will number 25 million by the year 2000. São Paulo is also the dynamic economic centre and the industrial heart of Brazil, a country which has achieved in the last decade the most spectacular economic growth in the third world. Evidence of its wealth abounds — in its modern high rise office blocks, in its glittering shop windows filled with luxury items, in its expensive residential suburbs. This book examines the other side of this economic 'miracle'. Through an analysis of working and living conditions of the vast majority of its people, it exposes São Paulo's misery and poverty. The book's message is that the acute problems faced by millions of São Paulo's inhabitants are the result of this headlong pursuit of economic growth based on rapid industrialisation. For the problems to be tackled effectively, the very structures of power will need to be changed.

São Paulo Growth and Poverty was written by a group of distinguished sociologists and economists attached to the Centro Brasileiro de Análise e Planejamento (CEBRAP). Since its inception in 1969, CEBRAP has perhaps become Latin America's leading independent social science research institute. In addition to its own research programmes, CEBRAP accepts commissions from other organisations. These have included a study of abandoned children in São Paulo, commissioned by the São Paulo State Tribunal of Justice, and a demographic study of Brazil (under the aegis of the United Nations) for World Population Year. *São Paulo Growth and Poverty* was produced at the request of the Commission for Justice and Peace of the Archdiocese of São Paulo.

It may seem strange at first glance that an official Catholic body should commission such a study and some mention must be made of the role of the Catholic Church in Brazil. Under an authoritarian political system which suppresses democratic freedoms, the Church has been for many years one of the very few institutions able to speak out in defence of human rights. These rights include not only the freedom from arbitrary arrest, detention and torture but also freedom of speech, organisation and assembly, the right to education, health and nutrition. *São Paulo Growth and Poverty* is an important contribution from the Church in Brazil towards the defence of such rights which the economic and social policies pursued by the Brazilian government render meaningless.

Not surprisingly the publication of *São Paulo Growth and Poverty* provoked some hostile reactions, particularly from those committed to Brazil's current political structures and economic course. At the beginning of September 1976 the CEBRAP office was one of the targets in a spate of bomb attacks claimed by the Brazilian Anti-Communist Alliance. The attack on the CEBRAP office came shortly after the publication of *São Paulo Growth and Poverty* and was a clear indication that the book was regarded by the extreme right-wing as 'subversive'. This view was shared by Colonel Erasmo Dias, then the São Paulo State Secretary of Public Security. In a remarkable press interview, he claimed that the bomb placed at the CEBRAP building was nothing more than a publicity stunt by a little known institution to gain attention for a book which he described as "essentially Marxist", offering no solutions, distorting reality and presenting to the outside world a false image of São Paulo. He added that "there are numerous bodies in São Paulo which deserve a bomb and they were not bombed." "This is my bible" he said, brandishing a heavily underscored copy of the book, "I read this book every day in order to get angry." *(Folha da Tarde,* 7 September 1976).

Nevertheless *São Paulo Growth and Poverty* became an immediate best seller and has run into several editions. It received extensive and excellent reviews in Brazil's leading newspapers and journals. Professor Maria Isaura Pereira de Queiroz, an eminent sociologist of international repute, wrote in *Ciência e Cultura,* "The seriousness of the research and the accuracy of the analysis demonstrate the high level which has been reached in the work of social science specialists in Brazil." *Veja,* the leading weekly news magazine, carried a review which said, "The apocalyptic visions in *São Paulo Growth and Poverty* are the result of a unique methodological approach. For the first time an attempt is made to think of São Paulo from the point of view of the conditions in which its inhabitants, and especially its workers, live."

We have commissioned and published an English translation of *São Paulo Growth and Poverty* because we believe that it will make an invaluable contribution to all those concerned with the problems of development and those striving for a more just and equitable society.

Catholic Institute for International Relations, London
July 1978

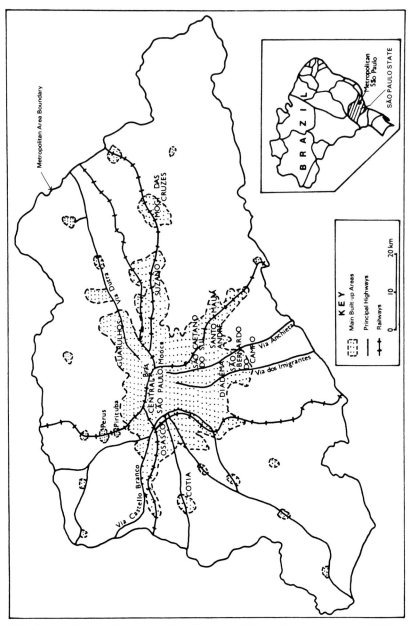

Map showing Metropolitan Area of São Paulo, including main transport routes, built-up areas, principal municípios, and selected districts (referred to in the text).
Also: Inset showing location of São Paulo state within Brazil and position of Metropolitan São Paulo.

Preface to the English edition

São Paulo: Growth and Poverty remains, almost two years after its publication in Brazil, completely up-to-date. Its original purpose was to provide a current, and therefore quickly dated, analysis of the conditions in which the people of São Paulo live. Its impact, however, on both academic and political circles, illustrates its continuing importance as an interpretation of the conditions of development of the city.

What is the point of translating into English a text dealing with the economic and social situation of São Paulo, Brazil? Several factors converge to transform this sociological essay into compelling and original reading which should be both provocative and relevant to overseas readers.

It is a book which unmasks and denounces the leading example of what has been called the 'Brazilian economic miracle'. Based on irrefutable facts and systematic interpretation, the book paints a true-to-life picture which starkly reveals the contradictions suggested by its title. Two images of São Paulo are superimposed: on the one hand the growing accumulation of wealth and on the other increasing misery and poverty. Official ideology and propaganda glorify the prosperity and turn a blind eye to the heavy human costs of this pseudo-progress. *São Paulo: Growth and Poverty* reveals what is hidden, what the ruling classes pretend not to know, what the tourists never see. The reality it describes, however, is at the heart of São Paulo—the scandalous misery of the many, which sustains the luxury and privileges of the few, and on whom its dynamic growth is based and from whom its prosperity is stolen.

The book's approach has proved eminently suitable for interpreting a perverse process of urbanisation in an underdeveloped country. Perhaps the focus of the book, the point of view of the poorest, is relevant for the analysis of many different areas, which are often studied by social scientists who fragment their subject and base their analyses on purely functional theories.

Last but not least, *São Paulo: Growth and Poverty* shows the rejuvenated face of the Church. The text was commissioned by the São Paulo Pontifical Commission for Justice and Peace and our archdiocese has assumed full editorial responsibility. This is a Christian work, a part of the pastoral work of the Church which, like Christ, is engaged in serving the downtrodden and participating in the liberation of the oppressed.

São Paulo, 10 January 1978
Paulo Evaristo, Cardinal Arns
Archbishop of São Paulo

Introduction

'The joys and the hopes, the griefs and the anxieties of the men of this age, especially those who are poor or in any way afflicted, these too are the joys and hopes, the griefs and anxieties of the followers of Christ. Indeed, nothing genuinely human fails to raise an echo in their hearts. For theirs is a community composed of men. United in Christ, they are led by the Holy Spirit in their journey to the kingdom of their Father and they have welcomed the news of salvation which is meant for every man. That is why this community realises that it is truly and intimately linked with mankind and its history.' *(Gaudium et Spes, No.1)*

Faithful to the spirit of the Council, the Commission for Justice and Peace of this archdiocese has sponsored an important study of the city of São Paulo and its peripheral areas. Once this initiative is in the hands of the public, we hope it will extend the horizon and deepen understanding of human rights. We hope that it will extend the horizon by dealing with the problems which confront the majority of the people, who are deprived of their most elementary rights. We hope it will deepen understanding by exposing the extent of the evils which afflict us and by seeking their origins so that they may be attacked and uprooted.

These studies, analyses and conclusions are not intended to exhaust their theme nor to be the final and definitive word on the reality of life in the country evangelised by Padre Anchieta. The facts and the ideas contained in this book merely suggest the re-opening of a wide-ranging debate and indicate some paths of action.

The vigorous growth of São Paulo, as demonstrated by the concentration of the means of production, of services, of capital — in a word, of wealth —

an unprecendented phenomenon in our country, goes hand in hand with the increase in poverty. São Paulo's development, in the light of the living standards of those who live here, has produced a wide and increasing gulf between the luxuries of a few and the hardships of the many. The deterioration in the living standards of the majority is dramatically illustrated by the inexorable path taken by the curve showing infant mortality. After steadily declining from 1940 onwards, when it fell by 30% between 1940 and 1950, and by 32% from 1950 to 1960, it abruptly reversed its course between 1960 and 1973 and increased by 45%.

It is a Bishop's mission to put into practice the message of salvation, repeating to his fellowmen the appeals of Christ and the Apostles. We invite the people of São Paulo to reflect upon this penetrating analysis of the problems of São Paulo which has been written by respected social scientists. No-one should feel exempt from its challenge. It is directed to all responsible people, of whatever nationality, race, ideology or creed. The appeal is most vehemently addressed to all those who hold positions of power in this city and to the lay-members of our Church. Underlying this challenge is the pressing need for action which our love for our neighbour demands of us. A Bishop, together with the whole Church, cannot in silence watch the widespread violence used against the people, cutting short lives through malnutrition and appalling health and sanitary conditions, through accidents at work and on the roads, through excessive work hours, fatigue and impoverishment, through lack of jobs and through wages which do not cover even basic necessities, through lack of housing and grossly inadequate public transport, through fear and the stifling of the rights of association, information and trade union activities.

In these times, however, it is not good enough merely to sympathise with the problems or to be moved by the misery and wretchedness, nor even to search for a palliative to offer those who knock at our door. It is not even enough that there are organisations dedicated to ameliorating the sufferings of the sick, the old, and the abandoned. We must actively seek the causes of these evils and organise ourselves to combat them with courage, patience and determination.

Can there be a logic behind such established disorder? We see a pattern of economic growth based on the destruction of the lives of workers obliged to labour excessive hours to compensate for the reduced purchasing power of their wages. What we offer those struggling to humanise the city and to change the conditions of people's lives is an X-ray of the reality of São Paulo accompanied by a diagnosis of the causes of this accumulation of misery.

By publicising these evils, will we be aggravating the problems and exasperating ordinary people? The facts are worrying but knowledge of them is an indispensable step towards finding acceptable solutions. Moreover, people are aware through their day-to-day experience, with the exactness and lucidity of those who have to struggle to earn their daily bread for themselves and their families, of the extent and seriousness of the problems. The barriers which prevent people from organising, participating and contributing to the solution of their problems and those of the city must be torn down. 'As long as the social and political initiative of the working classes continues to be blocked, it will be difficult to imagine São Paulo as a truly human city'.

Conscious of this task, the Church has drawn up its priorities for action. The Church is present in the most difficult areas of the periphery, working to integrate the people who have been dispersed and scattered. It attempts to be present in the work place, alongside those who suffer as they build the city sometimes at the cost of their lives. The Church is following the example of Christ and the Apostles, trying to take its place alongside those who are downtrodden and can find no justice, creating a base for the people to participate effectively at all levels of life and culture in the city.

It is here that the people's voice is to be heard. If we pay attention to it and listen to its cry, we shall see the signs of the time and hear the voice of God in contemporary history.

The way to avoid a depersonalised society may be through setting up small grass-roots communities, conscious of their rights and duties, and having their say in the decisions which involve the common good and hence the fate of the community.

Conscious that local Church groups and all those who are engaged in understanding the reality of São Paulo and the mechanisms which control this reality will reflect on, discuss, and transform the contributions made in this book into a revitalisation of the work of evangelisation and liberation, we present to them this study *São Paulo: Growth and Poverty,* expressing our gratitude to the social studies centre CEBRAP and to the Commission for Justice and Peace for their invaluable assistance.

São Paulo, 24 June 1976
Feast of St John the Baptist
Paulo Evaristo, Cardinal Arns
Archbishop of São Paulo

São Paulo and the Brazilian economy

The underlying purpose of this book is to survey current trends in the development of the Metropolitan Region of São Paulo from the point of view of the living conditions of its inhabitants. A systematic presentation of socio-economic facts about living conditions in São Paulo would be sufficient to illustrate the enormity of the problems confronting those who live in the metropolis. Any description of this kind, however, leads to questions about the nature of the society which gives rise to and perpetuates such living conditions.

When discussing the growth of São Paulo, mention must be made of the privileged position of its economy in relation to the under-development of other regions of Brazil. As the centre of economic activity of the richest state in the country, the area of Greater São Paulo has witnessed a considerable accumulation of wealth. In 1969, the latest year for which statistics are available, 35.6% of Brazil's domestic product was concentrated in the state of São Paulo. It is quite likely that this concentration of wealth has intensified during the 1970s due to the continued massive investments channelled into the state. Given that about 19% of Brazil's population lives in São Paulo state, income per head in the state is more than double that in the rest of the country.

At the same time, it is important to remember that the *per capita* income provided by agriculture in São Paulo state is the same as in the rest of the country, while that provided by manufacturing is some 5.4 times greater than in other parts of the country. Thus São Paulo performs a highly specialised function in the national economy. It is the centre of manufacturing, the sector of economic activity which has expanded the fastest of all. With 40% of the state's income provided by manufacturing, and only

12.4% by agriculture, São Paulo spearheads the industrialisation drive. The average income of the other states in the country reflects a different pattern, with manufacturing providing only 17.5% and agriculture 26.6%. Moreover, São Paulo accounts for a large proportion — 45.8% of national income from rents, which gives a rough idea of the high rental value of both its residential and its non-residential properties.

It cannot be concluded from the high concentration of wealth in São Paulo, however, that the population of the state as a whole is better off. Statistics relating to *per capita* income do not mean that all inhabitants receive an equal slice of the cake. They show only the quantity of income received in the state in relation to the number of people, without implying anything about the way it is distributed.

São Paulo's economic superiority is, to a great degree, based on ownership. Not ownership in general, but specifically the ownership of capital. As the country develops under its present economic system, it becomes increasingly capitalist, which means that a growing proportion of its means of production assume the characteristics of capital. In other words, we are talking about an economy in which the most important means of production are the property of non-producers, who administer them either directly or through representatives. Production is organised on the basis of companies, whose primary aim is to provide profits for their owners, and which grow either through the reinvestment of the profits themselves or through attracting the surplus generated by other economic sectors.

In addition to these companies, a part of overall production is in the hands of self-employed workers who own the means of production which they use. This category includes craftsmen, small traders and members of some of the liberal professions.

Then there is the so-called public sector, in which the means of production are owned by the state. This sector is partly made up of state companies which produce goods and services in accordance with the rules of the market economy. Apart from these companies, this category also includes sectors which are not strictly speaking productive, such as government departments, whether at the federal, state, or municipal level, also the armed forces, the civil and military police, those who work for the various legislative bodies and the courts, and those who provide social services — education, health, social welfare, etc. — paid for by the state.

In the region of Greater São Paulo, about 12.5% of the labour force consists of self-employed workers, while 1.6% are family members earning no income (they generally work for the head of the family). It is reasonable to estimate that 10% of the labour force in Greater São Paulo is employed in the public sector. Thus we may conclude that 76% of the total labour force works in the privately-owned companies, 72% as employees.

The process of growth in which capital expands by assimilating its own product—profit—is what is called capital accumulation. Even in 1948, São Paulo already held a dominant position in the process of capital accumulation and was responsible for no less than 45.9% of all capital issues in Brazil.[1] After a temporary fall during the first half of the 1960s, São Paulo's share again climbed to over 40% and in 1972 reached the remarkable figure of 44%. This means that capital in Brazil is highly concentrated in São Paulo, which receives resources for accumulation both from the rest of the country and from abroad. The state of São Paulo is responsible for 35.6% of domestic product and about 44% of capital accumulation. Comparing, for instance, total capital issues with domestic product in 1969, we get the following rates of accumulation: Brazil as a whole 22.6%, of which São Paulo 33.6%, and other regions of Brazil 16.7%. It does not seem very likely that the proportion of accumulated wealth produced in São Paulo is double that of the rest of the country. It is probable instead that a substantial proportion of the resources accumulated in São Paulo originates outside the state.

This regional concentration of income is the result of two factors. The first is the savings which accrue from the concentration of manufacturing and commercial activities in the same area. Energy, transport, telephones, water supply, sewage treatment, and so on, produced on a large scale, are cheaper per unit in São Paulo than in poorer and less industrialised states. The other factor is the capitalist nature of the development process in question. In Brazil as in other countries, capitalist development involves a growing concentration of capital. An analysis of the reasons for this tendency does not fall within the scope of this study,[2] but its results clearly

1. The best information available on capital accumulation in Brazil is that collected by the Getúlio Vargas Foundation on capital issues by corporations. Their statistics of the overall value of these issues do not reflect so much real investment, that is, the value of additions to the country's capacity to produce, as the value of additions to total capital. Thus, whenever a part of the means of production, even those already being used, becomes the property of a joint stock company, its value is included as part of Capital Issues, under the heading of 'New Companies'. Capital accumulation should not be confused with 'Gross Formation of Fixed Capital', as detailed in the National Accounts. In addition to accumulation properly speaking, the 'Gross Formation of Fixed Capital' also includes newly-built residential property and un-remunerated government activities (construction of reservoirs, airports, barracks, etc).

2. For an analysis of the effect of capital concentration on geographical distribution of economic activities, see Singer, P., *A Economia Política da Urbanização*, São Paulo, Brasiliense, 1973.

tend to reinforce the geographical concentration of income. In 1967 São Paulo was the site of 21 of the 50 biggest companies in the country. In 1973 this figure had risen to 26. To the extent to which the largest capitalist companies tend to grow faster than the others, this leads to a greater accumulation of resources in São Paulo.

The fact that São Paulo has established itself as the dominant centre of the process of accumulation in Brazil implies a relative impoverishment of other parts of the country. Apart from the direct transfer of resources for investment, another source of concentration results from the privileged position of the São Paulo economy in the regional division of labour. Since São Paulo brings together the most advanced sectors of industrial and agricultural production, the productivity of its companies is greater, thus giving it an advantage in its terms of trade with other regions.

An even greater contrast exists between the development of Greater São Paulo, including the Capital and surrounding districts, and the underdevelopment of other parts. Since it contains most of the state's industry and has remained in the forefront of the process of the concentration of wealth for several decades, Greater São Paulo has become a vast agglomeration, with a population of almost 11 million,[3] of which 96% live in urban areas. Although the growth of industry in other areas of the state has recently accelerated and although other parts of the country may experience higher rates of growth than Greater São Paulo, the gap that already exists between it and other Brazilian cities cannot easily be bridged.

The economic drive of São Paulo compared to other areas of the country can clearly be seen as much in the vast number of existing facilities (buildings, electricity supply, etc.), as in any of the indicators generally used to measure economic growth (industrial production, the financial system, *per capita* income, etc.). However, if the development of the city is examined from the point of view of the living conditions of its inhabitants, a great and increasing inequality is found between the riches of a few and the problems of the majority. It is the gap between the wealth evident in the sumptuous houses of the 'garden' areas of the city and the poverty of the working-class districts, which lack such basic urban amenities as transport, water, drains and proper housing. It is the contrast between the growth in the consumption of luxury items and the fall in the real value of the minimum wage.[4]

3. Estimate for 1975.
4. Translator's Note: The minimum wage is in theory the minimum which any adult worker should receive in order to be able to keep himself and his family. In practice it is insufficient to keep one person, let alone a family and, in any case, many workers, particularly women, receive much less.

The contrast between the degree of economic development of Greater São Paulo — as measured by overall levels of accumulation — and its growing poverty again raises the question of what is meant by the 'privileged position' of the metropolis. Even if it is true that malnutrition, unsatisfactory health standards and inadequate housing conditions, to mention just some of the symptoms of poverty to be found in the city, are worse in other regions, at least it should be clear that these 'problems of underdevelopment' do not automatically disappear with economic growth. On the other hand, as the facts examined in the following chapters show, poverty is not diminishing in São Paulo, but is in many ways tending to increase. The least that can be said is that the 'privileged position' of São Paulo applies to some people but by no means to everyone.

Many analyses made in the past tended to suggest that the undesirable effects of economic growth on the living conditions of city-dwellers in Brazil were confined to those in a marginal situation. From this point of view, urban poverty is a separate and specific aspect within the context of progress and well-being created by industrialisation and urbanisation. In contrast with rural misery, the poverty of the marginalised city-dweller is considered a fact of lesser importance, albeit undesirable, a temporary phenomenon characteristic of a period of geographical reorganisation of production. Often urban poverty has been regarded as a period of transition for migrants coming from rural areas before they are absorbed into the urban-industrial economy.

Research into internal migration and income differentials between migrants and non-migrants in Brazilian towns has brought to light evidence which differs radically from these suppositions.[5] It is apparent that there is no scientific basis for the notion that the social inequalities in question can be explained by reference to the division between migrants and the locally-born population. Moreover, when the huge contribution made by migrants to urban growth rates in recent decades is taken into consideration, it becomes clear that this division cannot explain particular situations. In the case of Greater São Paulo, as the latest (1970) census revealed, 52.5% of the population were "persons not born in the municipality where they reside" (see table 4). Looking at the families of these people as far as their first-generation descendants, it becomes apparent that the 'migrant population' accounts for more than two-thirds of the residents of the metropolis. This being the case, how can their living conditions be defined as residual problems?

5. See in particular, Mata M. da *et al*, *Migrações internas no Brasil*, Rio de Janeiro, IPEA-INPES, 1973.

Taking their cue from the international outcry over big city problems — pollution, transport difficulties, stress, loneliness — more recent intrepretations suggest that it is the process of development itself which is responsible for the inhuman conditions of 'modern' life. In the case of São Paulo, this view only makes sense given two assumptions. First, that the inhuman living conditions in less 'modern' parts of the country should not be taken into consideration. Second, that differences and inequalities between the inhabitants of the city should not be analysed but that the population should be considered as an undifferentiated whole.

In fact, it becomes clear from the analysis of the living conditions of the people of São Paulo that most of the problems they are up against do not stem from the city's growth as such. The problems differ according to social class and furthermore are the result of the ways in which production is organised and wealth distributed which are not peculiar to São Paulo. Working conditions and wages, in a population with an overwhelming majority of wage-earners, are the aspects which weigh most in determining the 'quality of life'. These aspects cannot be explained outside the context of the Brazilian economy as a whole. In their turn, economic relations are bolstered by a political system which defines the degree of participation of both individuals and classes in decisions concerning their own fate. Once again, it is not a question of something peculiar to modern city life but of a problem that must be placed in a wider context.

A picture of living conditions in the city of São Paulo also provides a more general view of the Brazilian economy and society. It is true that there are some aspects peculiar to the city's position in the overall context of Brazil. However from the point of view of the majority of the population, these peculiarities do not consist in the absence of problems which exist in other parts of the country. What is principally peculiar to São Paulo is perhaps the exaggerated contrast between wealth and poverty.

The logic of disorder

The intense economic growth of the city of São Paulo has been accompanied by a deterioration in the living standards of widespread sectors of its population. The links between the process of urban growth and the increase in 'urban problems' has become so clear that a few years ago, the mayor reversed the city's earlier proud boast that "São Paulo cannot stop!" and instead proclaimed "São Paulo must stop!". He was referring particularly to the ever-increasing shortfall in public works and services which was growing at an even faster rate than forecast by the planners. The mayor assumed that controlling the city's growth would make it possible to tackle its problems, a point of view that tends to attribute the inconveniences suffered by its population to the process of growth itself or to its rapidity.

The notion that the city's progress has a price which must be paid by its inhabitants has often been repeated in connection with the most varied of problems: from pollution of the environment to inadequate urban facilities, from transport difficulties to bad housing conditions, from insufficient leisure facilities to the rising crime-rate. The choice implicit in this approach — stagnation or sacrifice — is quite consistent with the ideology of development currently in vogue: if the country is to develop and the future happiness of its inhabitants to be assured, the people must forego the satisfaction of some of their needs in the present. At the same time, current problems are often attributed to the chaotic manner of the city's growth and to the absence or inefficiency of planning in the past. São Paulo, from this point of view, should not only pay the price for its future happiness but also atone for the damage caused by its improvidence in the past.

The disorderly appearance of the city as it grows can be seen on the map: its irregular outline and the random manner in which empty and occupied areas are distributed reflect the incoherent and random manner in which the land has been occupied. This impression of disorder is confirmed by something which does not show on the map: the 26,000 roads which have been built and the 5,000 estates which have been sold off in plots for individual houses without the permission of the municipal authorities. The surface disorder, however, tends to hide the social organisation of the city. Behind the 'urban problems' is the life of the city's residents which revolves around the sharing out both of the benefits of development and of the price which has to be paid for that development.

The conditions in which people live depend on a series of factors which are directly or indirectly linked to the system of production and distribution of wealth. For the population of São Paulo, the majority of which are wage-earners and their families, it is the organisation of work which is decisive. This is true in terms both of the conditions in which work is done and of the wages which are paid, which in turn determine people's access to available goods and services. In addition to the organisation of work, however, the very way in which land in the city is used and the amenities and services that are provided also determine people's quality of life.

Many of the items necessary to life in the city can be bought individually, such as food, clothing, furniture, household goods, books, cars, houses etc. The same is true of certain services, from individual medical treatment to the use of taxis, from haircuts to laundries, and so on. Access to these goods and services depends directly on the amount of money which the would-be purchaser has available, that is, on the distribution of income.

The use of certain services is collective, although access to them also demands individual payment: piped water and drainage, electricity, telephones, public transport, some forms of community entertainment and cultural activities, etc. Theoretically these are at the disposal of all who can afford to pay for them. But access to them is made easier or more difficult not only according to their price or charge but also according to the public or private investment needed to establish them. In most cases this investment is determined by its potential profitability or its 'viability'. This means that preference in providing these services is given to consumers who can be relied upon to pay for them.

On the other hand, there are a number of goods and services whose cost falls not on the individual consumer but on the community in the form of taxes: the construction and paving of roads and squares, parks, traffic control, refuse collection, street lighting and so on. Through the indirect mechanism of property valuation, these goods and services are also shared out unequally. Plots of land and houses cost more in areas with better amenities and property prices serve as a mechanism for reserving both the properties and the municipal services for those who can pay more. The geographical distribution of the population in the city is thus determined by the social position of the inhabitants, and in so doing reinforces existing inequalities. Many years ago, a shanty-town dweller wrote that the "shanty-town is the city's rubbish heap".[6] Nowadays, the term 'periphery', which is used to designate districts far removed from the centre, has in certain circles become synonymous with the idea of marginality and social rejection.

The aggravation of the problems which affect the quality of life in São Paulo does not affect the city as a whole. Particularly over the last three or four decades, the working population has been housed not only in the traditional slums and shanty-towns but in the peripheral districts which have sprung up and begun to expand. It is in these areas that the poverty of the city and its inhabitants is concentrated.

In the early years of industrialisation, in fact until the 1930s, many firms solved the problem of housing their workers by building (usually close to the factory) 'workers' estates' on which houses were let or sold to the workers. The houses were intended principally for skilled workers. This solution was viable as long as the size of the work force to be housed was relatively small. Moreover the low cost of land and of construction made it worthwhile for the firm to tie the worker down. In this way, the provision of a place to live reduced the cost of his subsistence and allowed his wages to be reduced. Hence the investment made by the firm in buying the land and building the houses paid for itself. Typical of those days were the districts of Brás, Mooca and Belém, where workers' houses surrounded the factories, and life was dominated by the "whistle of the textile mill".[7]

With the intensification of industrial growth, the number of workers increased rapidly. From the employers' point of view, the most important thing was an abundant and cheap labour force which would make it possible to produce a large surplus. One result of accelerating migration was the formation of a reserve pool of labour in the city, which thus made it unnecessary to tie the worker to a particular firm. In addition to this, the growth of the working population increased the demand for housing. At the same time, the value of sites both for factories and for housing rose so that companies no longer found it worthwhile to build workers' estates.

Consequently employers transferred the cost of housing (purchase, rent, maintenance) and of transport to the workers themselves, and the cost of

6. Jesus, C.M. de, *Quarto de Despejo: diário de uma favelada*, São Paulo, Livraria Francisco Alves, 1960.
7. See the contribution made by E.A. Blay to the 27th Annual Meeting of the Brazilian Society for the Advancement of Science, Belo Horizonte, 1975.

TABLE 1   GREATER SÃO PAULO:
PROPORTION OF PRIVATE HOUSEHOLDS SERVED BY
STREET LIGHTING (1970)

Municipalities	Households served by street lighting (%)
Arujá	47.6
Barueri	70.7
Biritiba-Mirim	46.8
Caieiras	73.4
Cajamar	63.1
Carapicuíba	77.1
Cotia	64.3
Diadema	82.1
Embu	56.9
Embu-Guaçu	39.0
Ferraz de Vasconcelos	74.6
Francisco Morato	54.0
Franco da Rocha	84.5
Guararema	41.0
Guarulhos	83.8
Itapecerica da Serra	34.5
Itapevi	66.3
Itaquaquecetuba	62.3
Jandira	73.0
Juquitiba	13.5
Mairiporã	55.7
Mauá	87.4
Mogi das Cruzes	81.7
Osasco	93.1
Pirapora do Bom Jesus	46.3
Poá	86.7
Ribeirão Pires	84.9
Rio Grande da Serra	57.4
Salesópolis	34.0
Santa Isabel	50.7
Santana do Parnaíba	45.5
Santo André	97.5
São Bernardo do Campo	92.7
São Caetano do Sul	99.8
São Paulo	95.7
Suzano	71.4
Taboão da Serra	81.0
Total in Region	*92.9*

Source: *VIII Recenseamento Geral — 1970. Censo Demográfico — São Paulo,* IBGE, Rio de Janeiro, 1973, vol. 1, section 18, 2nd part, pp.470-84.

basic urban services, where they existed, to the state. From then onwards workers' estates tended to disappear and the question of housing was instead determined by the laws of the property market. On the urban landscape a new feature appeared which was to become known as the 'periphery'. It consisted of housing estates, whether built with the municipal authorities' permission or not, that were devoid of basic facilities and inhabited by the workers needed to increase production.

Since accumulation of wealth and speculation go together, the geographical location of the working class was determined by the dictates of property interests.[8] Faced with the explosive growth of the metropolis, government authorities were slow to assume the legal powers necessary if they were to try and impose a minimum of order on land use. The first attempts in this direction occurred when the city had to a large degree already assumed its present appearance. As government action was almost always limited to servicing the residential centres created by the private sector, public investments were placed at the service of land speculators and builders.

Some figures: there are 4.5 square metres of green area for each inhabitant, when the minimum usually accepted is eight. Only 40% of the 8,000 kilometres which make up the road network for local traffic in the Metropolitan Region are paved.[9] Approximately 489,000 inhabitants live in houses without electricity.[10] Only about 30% of households in the Metropolitan Region have drains and only 53% have piped water. As a result, "in general people make use of open holes, dry lavatories and septic tanks... and drink water from shallow wells, which is usually contaminated by the proximity of the open holes".[11]

Even considering only the municipality of São Paulo, the lack of facilities is enormous. In 1968, as table 2 shows, 52.4% of households did not have piped water and 41.3% had no drains. Since then the situation has been deteriorating, especially on the periphery, where the shortage is even more dramatic: only 20% of houses have drains and 46% piped water. To give an

8. See J. Wilheim, *São Paulo Metrópole 65*, São Paulo, Difusão Européia de Livro, 1965.
9. São Paulo, Secretaria dos Negócios Metropolitanos, *Região Metropolitana de São Paulo: Diagnóstico 75. Condições Urbanas: Transporte*, São Paulo, 1975 (mimeo).
10. *PNAD — Regiões Metropolitanas, 4.° Trimestre 1971-1972*, Rio de Janeiro, IBGE, no date. See table 1 for variation between different municipalities; table 2 shows the shortfall in basic facilities in the districts which make up the Capital.
11. *Região Metropolitana de São Paulo: Diagnostico 75. Condições Urbanas: Saúde, op.cit.*, pp. 28 and 14-15 (mimeo). Translator's Note: 'dry lavatories' *(privadas secas)* are water-closets unconnected to any flushing or drainage system — they have to be regularly emptied by hand.

TABLE 2   MUNICIPALITY OF SÃO PAULO 1968:
HOUSEHOLDS LACKING BASIC SERVICES
(AS PERCENTAGE OF TOTAL HOUSEHOLDS)

Area	Water	Drains	Paved roads	Refuse collection
Centre	1.3	4.5	1.7	0.8
Ibirapuera	11.5	14.4	4.4	0.0
Pinheiros	30.0	49.2	29.5	16.8
Saúde	15.2	43.5	38.1	8.5
Ipiranga	20.1	29.2	40.5	89.9
Santo Amaro	49.9	61.1	56.8	19.0
Brás-Mooca	7.3	17.3	21.4	3.3
Santana	19.0	69.1	45.3	14.2
Lapa	29.3	46.4	75.3	9.1
Vila Maria	45.0	75.0	50.0	5.0
Tucuruvi	31.8	86.4	68.2	9.0
Casa Verde	51.3	81.1	46.0	8.1
Vila Prudente	30.0	57.5	62.5	12.5
Penha	43.2	74.4	70.3	59.8
Itaquera	89.3	96.9	87.5	71.9
São Miguel	49.9	44.4	44.5	11.1
Average	*52.4*	*41.3*	*34.3*	*15.9*

Source: *PUB*, São Paulo, 1968.

idea of the high degree of water contamination that exists, it is enough to
mention that three-quarters of households on the periphery "get rid of their
sewage into open holes, when not simply throwing it onto the ground."[12]
Even in many areas of the Capital, especially the south-east, north-east and
east, many roads are not paved and large areas have no lighting.[13]

The phrase, 'it's the price of progress' is put forward as a justification for
the shortcomings in the metropolis. However, this can hardly conceal the
failure on the part of the authorities to plan more rational forms of land use.
Moreover, given the weakness of grass-roots organisations and their inability
to intervene in the decision-making process, private enterprise has been
given ample freedom of action in its single-minded pursuit of profit.
"Property speculators ... thought up their own method of dividing up land
in the city. It worked as follows: a new site for a housing estate would never
be located immediately next to the previous one, which had already been

12. *Região Metropolitana de São Paulo: Diagnóstico 75. Desenvolvimento Sócio-Econômico,
   Promoção Social, op.cit.*
13. São Paulo, Prefeitura Municipal, *Plano Plurianual de Projetos CURA*, São Paulo, 1974.

TABLE 3 GREATER SÃO PAULO:
RATES OF POPULATION INCREASE,
THROUGH LOCAL BIRTHS, MIGRATION, AND TOTAL (1940-70)

Period and area	Through local birth		Through migration		*Total*	
	10-yearly	Annual	10-yearly	Annual	*10-yearly*	*Annual*
1950/1940						
Munic. São Paulo	15.8	1.48	49.9	4.14	*65.7*	*5.20*
GSP exc. Capital	8.3	0.92	83.8	6.26	*92.1*	*6.75*
GSP	14.7	1.38	55.1	4.58	*69.8*	*5.45*
1960/1950						
Munic. São Paulo	27.9	2.49	44.5	3.76	*72.4*	*5.60*
GSP exc. Capital	24.6	2.14	81.7	6.16	*106.3*	*7.50*
GSP	27.3	2.45	51.0	4.20	*78.3*	*5.96*
1970/60						
Munic. São Paulo	23.9	2.13	32.4	2.85	*56.3*	*4.54*
GSP exc. Capital	39.2	3.29	92.0	6.75	*131.2*	*8.70*
GSP	27.0	2.36	44.4	3.76	*71.4*	*5.50*

Source: CEBRAP, *Recursos Humanos da Grande São Paulo*, São Paulo, GEGRAN,
1971, vol. 1, p.63.

provided with public services. Instead, an area of empty land would be left between the new and the old site. Then, when the new site was sold off, the bus route put on to serve it would of course be an extension of the one serving the old site. By passing through the intermediate empty areas, however, the extended route immediately raised the value of the area. The same happened with other public services: to reach the new site, they would have to pass through empty areas, which would thus immediately benefit from the new facilities. In this way, public improvements would add to the value of the land, usually before it was occupied. Even today, if you go to one of the suburban centres — Santo Amaro, Penha, or wherever — and carry on towards the periphery, you can see the process: before reaching each estate, you will see an area which is still unoccupied".[14]

In addition to the process outlined above, which has been in evidence since the 1930s, industrial growth was taking place along the railways around the Capital: the Santos-Jundiaí line boosted economic activities in Santo André and São Caetano, while along the Central do Brasil line, small

14. Cardoso F.H. *et al.*, *Considerações sobre o Desenvolvimento de São Paulo: cultura e participação, São Paulo, CEBRAP, 1973* (cadernos CEBRAP, no.14), pp.9-10.

TABLE 4   METROPOLITAN REGION OF SÃO PAULO 1970–TIME OF
RESIDENCE IN MUNICIPALITY OF NON-LOCALLY-BORN PERSONS
(AS PERCENTAGE OF TOTAL MUNICIPAL POPULATION)

Municipality	Time of residence				
	Under 1 year	1-2 years	3-5 years	6 and more years	*Total*
Arujá	7.2	9.8	10.8	22.5	*50.3*
Barueri	11.8	14.2	13.7	29.4	*69.1*
Biritiba-Mirim	10.7	11.5	9.4	23.2	*54.8*
Caieiras	10.3	13.0	6.8	26.7	*56.8*
Cajamar	10.2	6.4	8.6	34.9	*60.1*
Carapicuíba	14.4	14.2	13.1	31.0	*72.7*
Cotia	8.8	9.1	8.5	21.6	*47.9*
Diadema	16.5	20.5	20.4	24.6	*82.0*
Embu	17.0	17.5	16.1	21.1	*71.7*
Embu-Guaçu	7.0	7.5	12.0	20.5	*47.0*
Ferraz de Vasconcelos	14.8	14.7	12.8	33.9	*76.3*
Francisco Morato	11.8	18.7	19.5	29.0	*79.0*
Franco da Rocha	11.0	7.3	8.5	43.0	*69.8*
Guararema	11.6	8.3	8.4	19.9	*48.2*
Guarulhos	9.8	12.7	13.1	21.9	*57.5*
Itapecerica da Serra	11.6	10.9	10.5	17.6	*50.6*
Itapevi	10.3	11.9	12.6	30.0	*64.8*
Itaquaquecetuba	11.1	11.2	12.4	30.8	*65.5*
Jandira	15.8	14.3	18.6	29.4	*78.1*
Juquitiba	5.2	2.6	4.7	11.4	*23.9*
Mairiporã	9.1	8.0	8.3	21.1	*46.5*
Mauá	9.5	14.1	16.7	32.9	*73.2*
Mogi das Cruzes	3.6	5.0	5.6	29.6	*43.8*
Osasco	8.3	11.0	12.0	37.6	*68.9*
Pirapora do Bom Jesus	10.4	12.6	9.4	20.1	*52.5*
Poá	7.0	11.2	11.4	37.1	*66.7*
Ribeirão Pires	8.4	8.9	10.8	36.0	*64.1*
Rio Grande da Serra	15.2	10.8	16.0	27.8	*69.8*
Salesópolis	4.4	2.3	1.5	10.1	*18.3*
Santa Isabel	5.7	5.1	5.4	13.5	*29.7*
Santana do Parnaíba	7.9	12.3	13.5	19.4	*53.1*
Santo André	5.8	7.5	9.0	43.4	*65.7*
São Bernardo do Campo	10.9	13.2	12.1	35.5	*71.7*
São Caetano do Sul	5.9	7.1	6.0	45.3	*64.3*
São Paulo	3.7	5.0	5.4	33.8	*47.9*
Suzano	7.6	9.5	12.0	36.7	*65.8*
Taboão da Serra	15.7	20.1	21.1	22.8	*79.7*
Metropolitan Region	5.1	6.6	7.0	33.8	*52.5*

Source: *VIII Recenseamento Geral — 1970, Censo Demogràfico — São Paulo*, IBGE, Rio de
Janeiro, 1973.

industrial centres were springing up and, more importantly, the so-called dormitory towns which from the beginning served firms in the Capital and, more recently, other industrial centres in the Metropolitan Region. After the Second World War and particularly after 1960, it was the turn of the roads, with São Bernardo and Diadema to the south-east, Guarulhos to the north, and Osasco to the north-west, passing at various times through a process of industrialisation. Each of these centres in turn created its own periphery.

The dizzy rate of growth of the population in the Metropolitan Region, no less than 5.5% per annum in the years 1960-1970, together with the process of withholding empty areas for speculative purposes, led to the growth of districts even further from the centre.[15]

The population of areas far removed from the work-centres, obliged to travel every day to work, grew rapidly. The springing-up of dormitory towns, in truth little more than camp-sites without any basic amenities, became predominant.[16] In addition to a job and a place to live, the question of transport in this context also becomes crucial.

"Those who work in Diadema don't live there. Those who live in Diadema don't work there", explains the mayor of that municipality, describing a situation which applies generally in Greater São Paulo.[17] For this reason, travelling to work becomes a chaotic business. In effect, the average travelling time has gone up by 30% over the last six years, while the distance travelled has also increased, especially for the workers using public transport: "bus-users who live on the periphery of the city ... (spend) 3 to 4 hours a day in the vehicles which take them to work and carry them back home".[18] Moreover, the problem of traffic jams has increased enormously in recent years, due to the rapid growth of the number of private cars — the

15. Migration played an important role in population growth in the Metropolitan Region: see table 3. For the proportion of non-locally-born persons and their period of residence in each municipality, see table 4.
16. It is worth pointing out that during the period under consideration the population in 12 of the 37 municipalities in the Region grew at a rate of over 15% a year. With the exception of Diadema and Guarulhos, the municipalities in question were just entering the process of industrialisation.
17. To give a few more examples: according to sources in the Osasco Local Authority, half of the active population works in other municipalties; 59% of the 102,000 employees in São Bernardo in 1973 lived outside the municipality. Again, it is estimated that around 100,000 people use the Via Dutra highway each day to get to their jobs in the Capital or in the industrial region known as 'ABC' (Santo André, São Bernardo and São Caetano). These examples have multiplied.
18. The figures quoted here are mainly taken from *Região Metropolitana de São Paulo: Diagnóstico 75. Condições Urbanas: Transporte, op. cit.*

total number of vehicles in the Capital increased from 120,000 in 1960 to almost one million in 1974. In 1968, a total of 7 million journeys were made daily, a figure which by 1974 had grown to 13.9 million. However, what should be stressed is the means of transport used. On the one hand there is individual transport: cars, for those who can afford them, carry on average 1.2 people each. Then there is public transport, with its 7,000 single-decker buses, not to mention a further 1,500 buses which run on inter-municipal routes. Every day the buses carry 6.8 million passengers: at the height of the rush-hour the load is about 130 passengers per bus, double the official maximum capacity. The suburban rail network, in its turn, transports 900,000 passengers a day. It's all in a day's travel for the 700 passengers who, twice a day, squeeze into trains that were built to take no more than 300.[19]

Obviously the 'traffic problems' affect everybody. Exasperation with traffic jams, blaring horns, lack of parking space, the tension that comes from driving around in a constant mass of vehicles, and, to a certain extent, the difficulty of covering ever-greater distances taking up an increasing amount of time, take their toll on those who use their own cars. But the toughest fate is reserved for the users of public transport, both in travelling to work and in going home afterwards.

Queues, overcrowding, delays, losing a day's work, and, at times, the anger which explodes into the stoning of trains and buses, cannot be dismissed as simple 'traffic problems'. The long hours spent waiting or travelling when one could be resting, whether before or after a long and arduous day's work, add daily to the exhaustion of those who have to use buses and trains to get to their jobs.

Although production requires that the work force turn up at the factories every day, the cost of this requirement, measured both in terms of fatigue due to travel and in monetary terms, is accepted as a problem only to the extent to which it affects production or labour productivity: "if the employee", as a Vice-President of FIESP, the Industrial Federation of São Paulo State, put it, "did not have to spend 3 hours travelling to work each day, which is what happens in São Paulo, he could produce more and save not only his own energy, but also that used in transporting him".[20]

Caught in an economic trap from which he cannot escape, the worker must, in order to continue to survive both as a wage-earner and as an urban

19. Translator's note: And for the *pingentes*, the more intrepid passengers, who, on finding the train too crowded to get in, travel hanging on to the outside. Regularly someone falls off and is killed.

20. *Região Metropolitana de São Paulo: Diagnóstico 75. Assentamento Industrial, op. cit.*

dweller, endure a wearying journey which further saps what he has to offer — his labour-power. Moreover, if he is unlucky enough to be counted among the lesser-skilled workers, whose labour is in abundant supply, his exhaustion is no loss to his employer, who can replace him once his productivity begins to decline.

It is easy to understand that, as a city grows, its borders expand and areas available for occupation are only to be found on the outskirts of areas already settled. It is not only this, however, that happens in São Paulo. When it comes to a place to live, workers are doomed to the periphery even if there are areas available which are nearer the centre or which are better provided with basic amenities. Moreover it is not only the latest arrivals who have to make their way to out-lying districts. Poorer people who live in older residential areas of the city are also pushed out as land values start to soar.

Public investments usually act as a stimulant to speculation in the central areas of the city when, for example, areas which have been left in a state of neglect receive investments in the form of services or basic facilities. The construction of a throughway, the channelling of a simple stream, in short, an urban improvement of any kind is immediately reflected in rising land prices.

The most obvious and recent example of this is to be found in the areas alongside the present and future course of the underground metro system. In the districts through which it runs it leads to changes in existing land use and type of property and pushes up the price of sites for sale. The area consequently assumes a different appearance because of its new role as a site for housing and services for the better-off, while poorer people are pushed out to more distant areas. Government compulsory purchase and official 're-urbanisation' schemes accelerate this process. In this way the public transport system, which should exist to meet the travel needs of the working population, becomes a means of furthering the interests of the more privileged.

The process of the expulsion of poorer people operates wherever land values are rising rapidly in the Metropolitan Region. The case of the Martinelli building is an example of the way in which areas are reclaimed for the middle class as the rise in property values becomes incompatible with the continuing presence of low-income sectors. The public authorities demand repair and restoration work, the cost of which is beyond the pocket of poorer residents, who are thus obliged to move out to areas on the periphery.

The same thing happens to a certain extent in the Capital's shanty-towns, which although not permitted by law to expand, at present house around

130,000 people. After the intense efforts to do away with shanty-towns during the 1960s, they have tended to spring up again in the wake of the development of the more industrialised parts of Greater São Paulo. Although overall statistics on the shanty-town population of Greater São Paulo do not exist,[21] it is known to be very numerous in certain municipalities — Guarulhos, Osasco, Diadema, São Bernardo do Campo and in the Capital — and displays similar socio-economic characteristics: the men are building labourers, odd-job men and unskilled industrial workers, while the women are almost exclusively employed in domestic service. In 80% of cases, the family income is no more than 2 minimum wages. Although shanty-town dwellers are usually migrants, 41.1% of those who come from other municipalities have lived in São Paulo for more than 5 years. Shanty-towns thus cannot be said to house only recent arrivals in the city.[22]

The location of the shanty-towns tends to follow the course of industrialisation, with shacks erected in areas close to the market for unskilled labour. As soon as the value of a privately-owned plot of land goes up, or the authorities wish to use the land where they have put up their shacks, the shanty-town dwellers are pushed out. When pressure from property dealers and the authorities in an area mounts, new shanty-towns spring up in neighbouring areas where the property market has not yet become so profitable. A typical example of this was the transference some years ago of the shanty-towns in São Caetano to Mauá, an obvious case of the 'cleaning-up' of an area where property values were rising rapidly.

In addition to the 130,000 shanty-town dwellers, there are 615,000 slum-dwellers in São Paulo. A further 1.8 million individuals live in very roughly-built houses on the periphery. These figures refer only to the Capital. Although there are no complete statistics, a similar situation is known to exist in other municipalities in the Metropolitan Region.

21. The latest data provided by the *PNAD* (National Household Sample Survey) indicate the existence in the Metropolitan Region of São Paulo of 54,739 shacks with 255,977 residents in the last quarter of 1971, and of 70,920 shacks with 318,285 residents at the end of 1972. Projecting the same rate of growth into more recent years, by the last quarter of 1975 there would have been some 590,000 inhabitants of Greater São Paulo living in shacks. Not all of them could strictly speaking be considered shanty-town dwellers, but these figures give an idea of the size of the problem. In the Capital, the shanty-town population in 1975 was estimated at 130,000 people, which represents 80% more than in the last survey carried out in 1973 by the municipal authorities.

22. See in particular *Estudo sobre o Fenômeno de Favelas no Município de São Paulo*, São Paulo, Secretaria de Bem Estar Social da Prefeitura do Município, 1974 *(habi-Coped* bulletin, Special Series, no. 1). The above figures refer to the Capital in 1973.

With the explosion in land prices, the tendency towards expelling poorer people to the periphery has accelerated. There, far from the work-place, shacks and roughly-built houses have mushroomed on plots of land hardly more than camp-sites and lacking even a minimum of facilities. In terms of the quality of both the buildings and the basic amenities, not to mention the legal aspect of the ownership of the land in question, the new working-class districts are not very different from the shanty-towns. The roughly-built houses on the periphery are 'owner-occupied', for the good reason that many working-class people had no alternative but to build there given the system of property speculation.

A little over half of private households in Greater São Paulo are houses which are owned by their occupants or are being bought by them (see table 5). This figure includes both the luxury houses and flats belonging to the

TABLE 5   GREATER SÃO PAULO
TYPE OF PRIVATE HOUSEHOLD (1972)

Type	No. of households		No. of residents	
	Number	%	Number	%
Owner-occupied	885,453	43.51	4,039,717	45.39
In process of acquisition	174,920	8.59	835,076	9.38
Sub-total	*1,060,373*	*52.10*	*4,874,793*	*54.77*
Rented	768,477	37.76	3,182,203	35.76
On loan and other	206,477	10.14	842,810	9.47
Total	*2,035,327*	*100.00*	*8,899,806*	*100.00*

Source: *PNAD, Regiões Metropolitanas, 4.° Trimestre 1971-72*, Rio de Janeiro, IBGE, no date, p.282.

middle class, which have either been built with the owner's own resources or acquired through the National Housing Bank (Banco Nacional de Habitação, usually known as the BNH) or other financing bodies. The indications are, however, that the majority of owner-occupied houses in São Paulo have been built by the owners themselves in their spare time after work or at weekends with the welcome help of relatives and friends. Although overall statistics are not available, a number of partial surveys indicate that this method of getting somewhere to live is common on the periphery of São Paulo.[23]

Building their own house is the only way less-skilled workers can get a

23. A study directed by Carlos Lemos, for example, showed that 88.5% of houses in the area of the periphery under survey had been built by their occupants. See *Opinião* newspaper, no.141, 18 July 1975.

place to live, in view of the fact that their wages are too low to enable them to pay rent, much less apply for a mortgage from the Housing Finance System (Sistema Financeiro de Habitação). On the other hand, this solution to the housing problem helps to keep down the wages paid by employers to their workers.[24] When an important item such as housing is subtracted from the living expenses of the workers, wages can be limited to covering the other essential costs such as transport and food.

Owning a house tends to tie the worker to a certain district. However, the process of economic development which gives rise to the peripheral districts also demands a greater degree of labour mobility.[25]

Travel between home and work thus becomes lengthier. In this way, the transformation of workers into home-owners has itself given rise to additional problems.

If the security of owning one's own home compensates in part for the insecurity experienced by workers in relation to their jobs, the comforts provided by their homes are far from making up for the attendant difficulties. The average number of occupants per habitable room in houses on the periphery of the Capital is 1.85 for groups whose family income is 3 minimum wages or less (78% of the total population), and 1.58 for families earning from 3 to 6 minimum wages (19% of the population).[26] However, when the number of persons per bedroom is calculated, the average for the whole of the Metropolitan Region reaches 2.6 — an acceptable standard would be one or two persons per bedroom (see table 6).

Housing conditions are even worse for the 615,000 slum-dwellers who live mostly in the run-down areas of the more central districts — Bom Retiro, Brás, Bela Vista. As these areas are rebuilt, the slums tend to spread into other cheap areas, especially those alongside the railways, for example, Perus and Pirituba. The average number of residents per room in the slums is 3.6. A quarter of the rooms have no outside windows. By way of compensation, 67% of slum-dwellers spend less than half an hour travelling to their place of work.[27]

24. An analysis of the connection between own-house building and the degree of exploitation of the labour force, and the way it fits in with the needs of capital accumulation, is made by F. de Oliveira in 'A Economia brasileira: crítica à razão dualista', in *Estudos CEBRAP* (2), São Paulo, October 1972, p.31.

25. In the state of São Paulo, labour turnover in industry and commerce was just over 50% in 1970, according to Ministry of Labour statistics.

26. See *Aspirações com relação a programa de Educação de Base, Caderno SEBES,* 1973.

27. Figures quoted here are taken from *Diagnóstico sobre o Fenômeno dos Cortiços no Município de São Paulo,* São Paulo, *HABI-SEBES,* 1975. 90% of slum-dwellers take less than an hour to get to work, in contrast with the much longer time taken by those living on the periphery.

TABLE 6 GREATER SÃO PAULO
AVERAGE NUMBER OF RESIDENTS PER BEDROOM (1970)

Municipality	No. of residents	No. of bedrooms*	Residents per bedroom
Arujá	8,972	3,174	2.8
Barueri	36,889	11,293	3.2
Biritiba-Mirim	8,853	3,204	2.7
Caieiras	14,089	5,058	2.7
Cajamar	10,215	3,678	2.7
Carapicuíba	51,900	16,558	3.1
Cotia	28,244	10,383	2.7
Diadema	75,544	22,028	3.4
Embu	17,457	5,355	3.2
Embu-Guaçu	9,120	3,285	2.7
Ferraz de Vasconcelos	23,645	7,319	3.2
Francisco Morato	11,091	3,327	3.3
Franco da Rocha	21,310	7,644	2.7
Guararema	12,085	4,482	2.6
Guarulhos	225,377	73,630	3.0
Itapecerica da Serra	23,471	8,115	2.8
Itapevi	26,686	8,200	3.2
Itaquaquecetuba	27,336	8,417	3.2
Jandira	11,770	3,435	3.4
Juquitiba	6,427	2,322	2.7
Mairiporã	18,829	6,792	2.7
Mauá	98,228	29,739	3.3
Mogi das Cruzes	135,798	48,629	2.7
Osasco	274,235	91,138	3.0
Pirapora do Bom Jesus	3,504	1,458	2.4
Poá	31,054	10,072	3.0
Ribeirão Pires	28,215	9,941	2.8
Rio Grande da Serra	7,564	2,444	3.0
Salesópolis	9,032	3,238	2.7
Santa Isabel	16,577	6,044	2.7
Santana do Parnaiba	5,125	2,144	2.3
Santo André	404,140	148,038	2.7
São Bernardo do Campo	191,864	68,847	2.7
São Caetano do Sul	145,366	55,963	2.5
São Paulo	5,641,330	2,239,201	2.5
Suzano	53,013	18,118	2.9
Taboão da Serra	39,156	11,590	3.3
Greater São Paulo	7,753,509	2,964,301	2.6

Source: *VIII Recenseamento Geral — 1970. Censo Demográfico* — São Paulo, IBGE, Rio de Janeiro, 1973.
*Including other rooms used as bedrooms.

Shanty-towns, slums and roughly-built houses on the periphery constitute the basic housing of the working classes and are a clear reflection of the inadequacy of their wages. Moreover, this situation has tended to deteriorate as real wages have fallen. To cover basic minimum expenditure on food, housing, transport, clothing, etc., a worker earning the minimum wage in 1975 needed to work 466 hours and 34 minutes a month, or 15 hours and 55 minutes a day, 30 days a month. To put it another way, if the minimum wage in 1970 was worth 100, four years later its value had fallen to 82. According to calculations made by the Inter-Trade Union Department of Statistics and Socio-Economic Studies (DIEESE), for the minimum wage in 1975 to regain the value it had in 1958 its nominal value would have had to be cr$1413.00, not cr$532.80; and its annual adjustment in 1975 would have had to be of the order of 275% and not a little over 40% as in fact it was.[28] The significance of these figures becomes apparent when it is remembered that in Greater São Paulo, around 19% of employees earn up to one minimum wage a month, 54% up to 2 minimum wages, and 75% up to three.

Apart from substandard housing conditions, the long working day and the several hours spent travelling to and from work, low wages are also associated with inadequate nutrition and a high risk of premature death.

From 1940 to 1950, the infant mortality rate in the Metropolitan Region fell by 30% and in the following decade by a further 32%. By contrast, in the 13 years up to 1975 it rose by 45%. It is well known that the main causes of infant mortality are associated with infectious diseases, which are themselves directly related to a lack of sanitary facilities and to undernutrition, factors which are generally associated with one another. With regard to sanitary facilities, which have already been discussed, it is worth mentioning that the proportion of the population of the Capital which receives piped water fell from 61% in 1950 to 56% in 1973, while the proportion with drains remained stable at around 35%. However, with respect to the Metropolitan Region as a whole, whereas in 1971 35% of the population had drains, four years later that figure had fallen to 30%.[29] With regard to eating habits, an official report states: "In lower-income classes, food consumption, in addition to diminishing in a quantitative fashion,

28. DIEESE monthly bulletin, São Paulo, April 1975.
29. *Região Metropolitana de São Paulo: Diagnóstico 75. Condições Urbanas: Saúde, op cit.,* p.5. Life expectancy at birth in the municipality of São Paulo was 62.3 years in 1959/67, but 60.8 years in 1969/71: that is, it fell by a year and a half. For changes in both infant and general mortality rates in the Capital and the other municipalities of Greater São Paulo, see graphs 1 and 2.

GRAPH 1 GREATER SÃO PAULO
CHANGES IN INFANT AND GENERAL MORTALITY RATES
(1940-70)

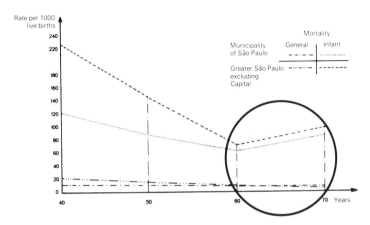

Source of data: CEBRAP, *Recursos Humanos da Grande São Paulo,* São Paulo,
GEGRAN, 1971, vol. 1, p.74.

GRAPH 2 GREATER SÃO PAULO
CHANGES IN INFANT MORTALITY RATES
(1960-70)

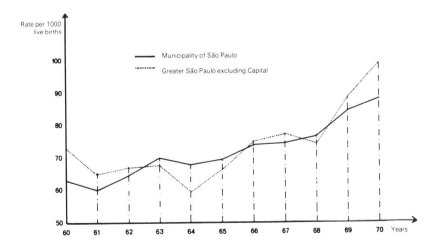

Source of data: CEBRAP, *Recursos Humanos da Grande São Paulo,* São Paulo, GEGRAN, 1971, vol. 1,
p.74.

consists of foodstuffs of inferior quality or type which cost less ... The reduction in purchasing power (fall in the real value of wages) has a marked effect on the eating habits of the poorer classes ... Malnutrition can be the direct cause of death or act as the most important aggravating factor on infectious diseases, thus increasing the rate of infant mortality". 52% of the population of the Capital and 73% of that of other municipalities in the Region suffer from undernutrition.[30]

The picture of general health conditions that has been painted here takes on an even more sombre hue in the light of the fact that a considerable proportion of workers do not have access to social welfare benefits. Leaving aside the 490,000 self-employed workers living in Greater São Paulo in 1972, the great majority of whom do not have employment and health insurance cards, it is known that no more than 70% of wage-earners have their cards in order. Taking men only — since female workers are to a large extent restricted to domestic service — the proportion who do not have cards in order is 20%.[31] And of those who did go to the National Institute of Social Welfare (INPS), the Brazilian national health service, in 1974 40% of the cases were not dealt with. In other words, a total of 4 million consultations that should have taken place did not. This situation indicates the state of neglect to which even registered workers are condemned when they are made redundant, are ill or have an accident at work, possibilities which are always present for a considerable number of those who depend solely on their labour to earn their living.

Again, consider the sharp increase in industrial accidents in Brazil. In this respect, the state of São Paulo is responsible for a high proportion of accidents: 712,000 in 1973, and 780,000 in 1974, figures which approximate to a quarter of the total of registered workers. This proportion is alarming when it is realised that in France, the proportion is three times less.[32]

30. *Ibid.*, p.19. Malnutrition appeared as a basic or associated cause in 28% of deaths of children of less than one year old in Greater São Paulo; leaving aside deaths at time of birth, the proportion rose to 45%. Again, 65% of cases of infectious diseases registered in the area were associated with malnutrition: *Investigação Interamericana de Mortalidade na Infância, Distrito de São Paulo, 1968/70*. Data concerning malnutrition and income levels are compared in table 7 and graph 3. Table 8 shows expenditure on food as a proportion of total family expenditure by income group.
31. *PNAD. Regiões Metropolitanas, 1°. trimestre de 1971-1972*, Rio de Janeiro, IBGE, no date, p.256. Translator's note: without cards, one cannot claim the right to medical treatment from the INPS.
32. *Região Metropolitana de São Paulo: Diagnóstico 75. Desenvolvimento e Inovações Tecnológicas, op. cit.* In the state of São Paulo, the number of accidents per working day has been increasing at an annual rate of almost 10%.

TABLE 7 MUNICIPALITY OF SÃO PAULO:
NUTRITION LEVELS FOR WORKING POPULATION
BY FAMILY INCOME (1969-70)

		Level of family income		
Nutrient	Average	Up to 3.0 minimum wages	From 3.1 to 6.2 minimum wages	6.2 minimum wages and above
Calories	99.8	91.1	100.6	109.6
Proteins	95.5	86.2	95.4	108.1
Calcium	50.8	41.9	50.0	65.4
Iron	107.1	101.0	107.6	114.3
Vitamin A	36.0	26.2	35.6	49.8
Thiamin	74.3	72.0	74.3	77.4
Riboflavin	63.0	53.9	62.0	77.6
Niacin	110.2	95.7	110.2	128.6
Ascorbic Acid	77.8	56.3	79.1	104.0
Overall nutrient profile*	Good	2	4	5
	Bad	2	1	2
	Very bad	5	4	2

Source: DIEESE, 'Família assalariada: padrão e custo de vida', *Estudos Sócio-Econômicos (2)*,
January 1974.
*Levels: Good — over 95.0
Bad — from 75.0 to 94.9
Very bad — below 75.0

GRAPH 3 PROPORTION OF CHILDREN AGED FROM 6 MONTHS TO 5 YEARS
SUFFERING PROTEIN/CALORIE DEFICIENCIES,
ACCORDING TO FAMILY INCOME
(IN *PER CAPITA* MINIMUM WAGES)

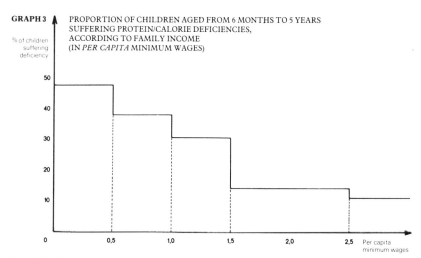

Source of data: Iunes M. *et al.*, *Estado nutricional de Crianças de 6 a 60 Meses no Município de São Paulo*, São
Paulo, Institute of Preventive Medicine of the São Paulo School of Medicine and Institute of Economic
Research of the University of São Paulo, 1975.

TABLE 8   MUNICIPALITY OF SÃO PAULO:
EXPENDITURE ON FOOD AS PROPORTION OF TOTAL FAMILY
EXPENDITURE, ACCORDING TO INCOME GROUP (1971-1972)

Income group*	1	2	3	4	5	6	7
No. of families as % of total	0.95	5.45	45.41	13.40	9.00	5.88	4.66
Monthly expenditure on food in cruzeiros	131	200	352	486	553	636	618
Expenditure on food as % of total family income	51.9	51.3	44.0	37.1	35.1	32.9	27.0

Source: Kirsten J.T. *et al.*, *Orçamentos familiares na cidade de São Paulo: 1971-1972*, São Paulo,
IPE-USP, 1973 (IPE Monograph series, no. 3).
*Translator's note: The income groupings used in this table are not based on the minimum
wage but on J.T. Kirsten's own scale.

When some 4,000 industrial accidents in São Paulo were analysed in
detail 23% were attributable to human error, while of the remainder, "there
was a safety failure which was either the cause itself, or was associated with
the cause".[33] Accidents are the result not only of safety conditions at work
but also of the fatigue inherent in industrial work and aggravated by long
working hours and the conditions to which workers are subjected outside
work, such as the time spent travelling to work, undernutrition and their
state of health. Over half the number of accidents occur to the upper limbs.
According to Ministry of Labour officials, the use of gloves could reduce
accidents by 22%. There is no reason to doubt this. However, in-depth
interviews illustrate another aspect of the recent industrialisation process.
Workers in one shop in a particular factory have to solder a certain number
of spots on a sheet which stops in front of them for a fixed period of time. If
they make a soldering error, the sheet does not count towards their total.
The average number of sheets to be soldered each hour is determined by a
time and motion study and a minimum level based on the performance of
the more dexterous workers is established. These workers can do their job
wearing gloves. The others however cannot and work without gloves. If they
injure themselves, they are fined. At times a worker suffers a total or partial
loss of nails and fingers. This situation came to light in a modern and
dynamic multi-national company in São Paulo. Other examples could be
given of similar working conditions which led to similar results.

33. Survey carried out by Leda Leal Ferreira. The results were partly published in the
weekly newspaper *Opinião*, no. 141, 18 July 1975.

Income group*	8	9	10	11	12	13	*Total average*
No. of families as % of total	2.19	2.51	1.97	1.38	4.08	3.02	*100.0*
Monthly expenditure on food in cruzeiros	677	772	781	787	832	1,095	*466*
Expenditure on food as % of total family income	27.1	28.1	28.7	25.1	21.2	16.7	*31.5*

The facts concerning both working and living conditions point to a deterioration in the situation of working-class families in São Paulo in recent years. Obviously not everybody has been affected to the same extent. The recent process of economic development has led to impoverishment not only in relative but also in absolute terms for widespread sectors of the working classes. On the other hand, the considerable accumulation of wealth over the same period has benefitted certain sectors of the industrial working class, especially skilled workers who, because of the development and diversification of industry, have managed to increase their wages and to participate if only in a limited way in the benefits of an industrial society.

Despite the existence of poverty and the deterioration in urban living conditions, moving to Greater São Paulo has meant both economic and social improvement for many migrants from other parts of Brazil. The facts show, however, a fall in the levels of basic consumption for workers as a whole. If many still think that 'things have got better', this view may result from an impression of participation which exists more at an imaginary than at a real level. Through the means of communication, mass society forges what could be called the market-place of illusions, the world of windows, television and bill-boards, in which those who have bettered themselves are presented as a source of hope for those who can only ever dream of becoming consumers.

The contrast between the sophisticated level of consumption of a small minority and the inadequate living conditions of the majority is tending to sharpen. Over the last 15 years, the model of industrial expansion has been based precisely on the production of consumer durables and luxury items. Although excluded from this particular market, the lower classes nevertheless paid a high price to make it possible. The living conditions of

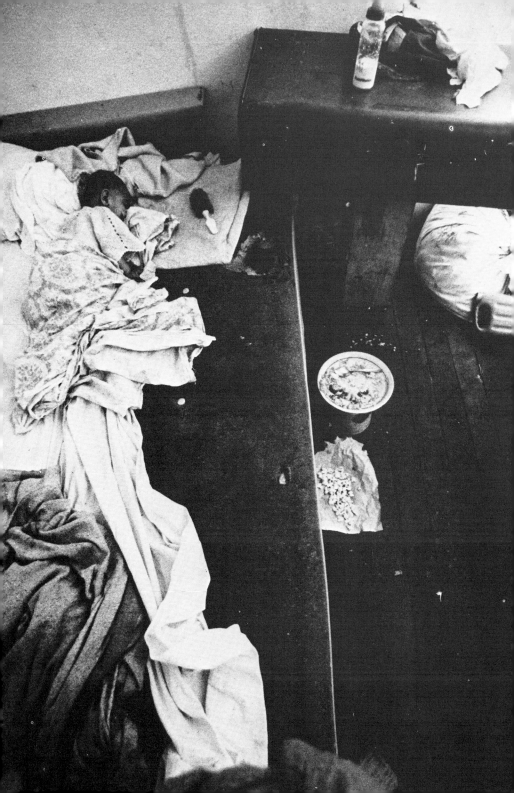

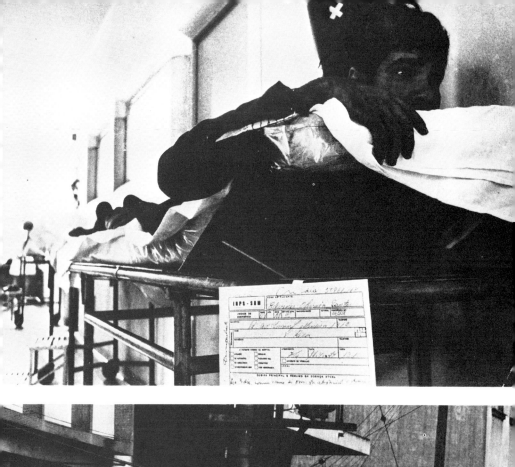

the majority of the working class deteriorated even faster during the very period when the economy of the country was expanding at the remarkable annual rate of 10%, which was widely labelled 'the Brazilian miracle'. But what kind of miracle is it which makes development synonymous with lowering the living standards of the majority of the population?

The rationale of the accumulation process to which recent development in Brazil has been subordinated is based directly on bleeding dry the working classes. Given the vast pool of reserve labour and the absence of solid trade union and political organisations among the working class, it has been easy to increase the rate of exploitation. The exhaustion of an underfed labour force through excessive working hours and harsh urban living conditions is possible because on the whole there is no problem in replacing it.[34]

From the point of view of the employers, for whom profit is the primary objective, this logic is impeccable. Moreover, it is not only among private companies that it prevails. The case of the publicly-financed building sector is instructive: 80% of loans granted by the National Housing Bank are channelled into buildings for middle and high income sectors, while the few housing schemes for low income earners have collapsed. Although people earning up to 4 minimum wages constitute 55% of housing demand, most residential properties placed on the market by the Housing Finance System have been intended for families earning more than 12 minimum wages.[35]

What happens in the housing sector also occurs in the urban planning and road building sectors. It has already been pointed out that the São Paulo local government authorities follow in the wake of land speculators, providing basic services, whether well or badly, in areas that have been occupied. When a few years ago, a road plan for the city as a whole was finally drawn up, it might have been thought that the interests of the community would prevail. On the contrary, however, the vast investments in building new roads, express throughways and elevated highways, have principally been intended to cater for the soaring number of private cars, with their one or two passengers, to the detriment of the public transport services which are used by the majority of the people.

In a situation in which the demands and protests of the community are forbidden, the problems experienced by people generally only become 'public problems' if they are shared by the ruling sectors. It could be said that air pollution, although concentrated mainly in industrial areas, nevertheless affects everybody. Again, although there exists a clear

34. In 1973, skilled workers in industry represented only 18% of employees in the sector: *Relatório SENAI,* São Paulo, 1974.
35. See table 9 for housing demand by level of income in the municipality of São Paulo.

TABLE 9 MUNICIPALITY OF SÃO PAULO:
HOUSING DEMAND BY LEVEL OF INCOME

Number of minimum wages	% of total demand
Up to 2	21.43
2 to 4	34.01
4 to 6	17.46
6 to 8	15.45
8 to 12	6.32
12 to 20	3.44
20 to 28	1.45
28 or more	0.15

Source: *Plano Plurianual de Projetos CURA* (1974), *op.cit.*

correlation between poverty and meningitis and the virus is selective, it lives in the air and can potentially affect everybody or at least frighten everybody. Everyone also suffers from the traffic to a certain extent. Undernutrition and industrial accidents, however, are not 'democratic' and it is clearly the working class that suffers from them. Nevertheless, few are the voices that are raised in protest, in spite of the great harm that is done. These problems appear secondary because they are not experienced directly by the ruling groups, and because the sectors they directly affect do not have the power to transform 'their' problem into a problem for the whole community.

The state of physical exhaustion to which the labour force is subjected could equally be transformed into a 'public problem' because of the negative effects it has on capital accumulation, to say nothing of social considerations which should stand above economic systems. While it may be profitable for the individual employer to destroy workers who can easily be replaced, for the employing class as a whole, the cost could prove heavy. The multiplication of social, environmental and physical problems brought about by the deterioration in the life of the city could eventually require the draining of resources which might otherwise be directed into productive investments. For the time being businessmen do not seem to be overly worried by this prospect and the government prefers to concern itself with stimulating the search for private profits.

As long as the social and political initiative of the working classes continues to be blocked, it is difficult to imagine São Paulo as a truly human city. For it is capital — and not labour — which is destroying life in the city. For capitalists, the city is a source of profit. For workers it is a way of life.

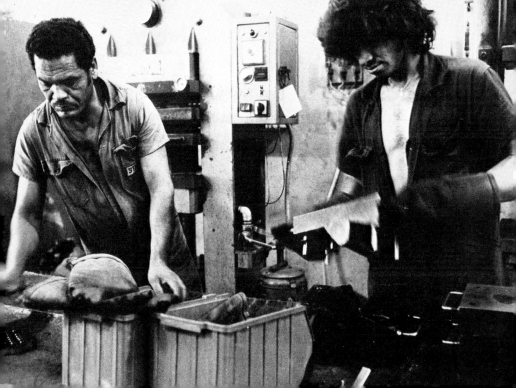

Accumulation and distribution

The contrast between the amount of material wealth produced in São Paulo and living standards of the city's inhabitants raises the question of how income is distributed among the different strata of society. This question involves the way in which the economy grows, or, more precisely, the process of capital accumulation.

Income distribution is not a 'social problem' together with all the other problems. The fact that infant mortality, nutrition standards, schooling, housing, hygiene, transport and leisure opportunities are unequally distributed among the city's inhabitants occurs because the resources needed to pay for people's various needs are also divided unequally. Moreover, if economic growth has not brought a corresponding improvement in living standards for the majority of the people, that is due to the very way in which the increase in wealth has taken place.

The pattern of income distribution is not decided after the wealth has been produced. In an economy based on commodity production, each product must have a buyer; in other words, a sum of money corresponding to the value of each product must be in the hands of someone who is in a position to spend it. The organisation of the productive process itself determines the way in which the wealth produced is distributed between wages and profits.

For an economy to grow, it must produce more than is needed to replace what was used up in the productive process in terms both of raw materials and equipment, and the physical effort of the work force. The surplus obtained, measured in terms of some unit of value, can be used to increase production with the employment of more machines, more raw materials, more workers etc. Alternatively it can be used to improve the consumption of the workers by raising wages, or of the employers by diverting more into profits. Thus, from a theoretical point of view, the growth of the economy can result in a wider distribution or a greater concentration of income, depending on the existing pattern of accumulation.

From 1968 onwards, the Brazilian economy entered a phase of accelerated growth which resulted in expansion of the Gross Domestic Product at a rate of 10% per annum. This rate of expansion was maintained until 1974. However, the gradual increase in domestic production, far from bringing about an improvement in general living standards, led principally to a strengthening of companies' profitability. Indeed, given that production per worker (labour productivity) grew from 1968 onwards at rates of over 5% a year, while the real value of the minimum wage was subject on the whole to negative rates of growth,[36] companies were able to appropriate all the gains obtained from productivity and thus increase the size of the surplus.

TABLE 10   DISTRIBUTION OF INCOME IN BRAZIL

% of population	% of total income	
	1960	1970
A. Top 1% on income scale	11.7	17.8
B. Following 4%	15.6	18.5
C. Following 15%	27.2	26.9
D. Following 30%	27.8	23.1
E. Bottom 50%	17.7	13.1

Source: Duarte J.C., *Aspectos da distribuicão da renda no Brasil em 1970*, Piracicaba, ESALQ-USP, 1971.

In the case of wages, salaries, and other forms of personal income, on the other hand, recent years have seen an intensification of the trend towards concentration. Though inequality in income distribution was already obvious in 1960, with the top 5% of the population receiving a proportion of total income (27.3%) well above the share of the 50% with the lowest incomes (17.7%), by 1970 this inequality had become even more accentuated: 5% of the population took home 36.3% of total income, a share virtually the same as that of the poorest 80% (36.2%). A breakdown of the figures shows that in 1970, the share of the top 1% of the population (17.8%) was well above that of the 50% with the lowest incomes (13.1%).

The recent trend towards income concentration is even more clearly

36. It is perfectly legitimate to compare labour productivity with the minimum wage, since more than half of the population enjoys a monthly income of one minimum wage or less (see table 11).

TABLE 11 DISTRIBUTION OF INCOME IN BRAZIL

Income in minimum wages	% of population with monetary income 1970	1972
Less than 1	50.2	52.5
From 1 to 2	28.6	22.8
From 2 to 3	10.2	9.8
From 3 to 7	7.1	9.4
From 7 to 10	1.7	2.3
More than 10	2.2	3.2

Source: Singer P., 'Mais pobres e mais ricos,' *Opinião* newspaper, no. 116, 24 January 1975.

illustrated when the population is divided into income levels on the basis of the minimum wage. From 1970 to 1972, the already high proportion of workers who receive less than one minimum wage increased from 50.2% to 52.5% of those receiving a monetary income. At the same time, an increase also occurred in the proportion receiving more than 3 minimum wages. Hence the proportion of the population which fell into the intermediate strata receiving between one and three minimum wages decreased and the two opposite tendencies could be observed. 3.9% rose on the income scale while 2.3% went down. The trend revealed by these figures is one of "a growing wealthy and well-off minority, at the same time as a growing and wretched majority".[37] Indeed, if the trend observed between 1970 and 1972 were to persist, "by 1980 we would have over 60% of the population earning less than one minimum wage, and around 30% earning over 3 minimum wages".[38]

Comparing the figures for Greater São Paulo with those for Brazil as a whole, we see that the proportion of those receiving less than one minimum wage is considerably smaller in the Metropolitan Region (see graph 4.). Consequently, the proportion of those in the intermediate and higher strata is comparatively greater in Greater São Paulo.

This relatively privileged position results from the location of many of the most dynamic sectors of the Brazilian economy in São Paulo, and consequently both wages and profits tend to be higher there than in the rest of the country. More than 30% of all those who receive a monthly income of over 5 minimum wages live in Greater São Paulo. This comparative

37. Singer, P. 'Quem são os ricos no Brasil', *Opinião* newspaper, no.119, 14 February 1975,
38. *Ibid.*   pp.11-12.

62 São Paulo: growth and poverty

GRAPH 4 INCOME DISTRIBUTION IN GREATER SÃO PAULO AND IN BRAZIL
(AS PERCENTAGE OF TOTAL POPULATION, INCOME BEING MEASURED IN
NUMBER OF MINIMUM WAGES)

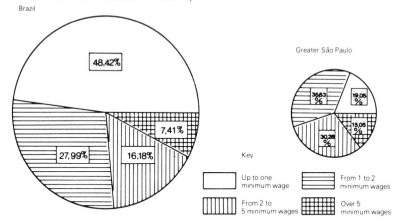

Source of data: *PNAD, Regiões Metropolitanas, 4.° trimestre, 1971-1972,* Rio de Janeiro, IBGE, no date.
Note: Distribution was calculated using the following items: monthly wages of employees paid in cash only;
monthly wages of employees paid both in cash and goods; employers and self-employed workers in
non-agricultural activities. The graph does not include data concerning employers and self-employed
workers in agricultural activities.

GRAPH 5 CHANGES IN REAL VALUE OF MINIMUM WAGE IN SÃO PAULO
(DECEMBER 1958 TO MAY 1975)

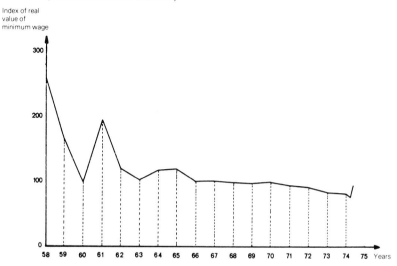

Source of data: DIEESE, in *Jornal da Tarde* newspaper, 30 April 1975.

GRAPH 6 CHANGES IN NUMBER OF HOURS OF WORK NEEDED TO
ACQUIRE MINIMUM ESSENTIAL DIET, 1965-75.
(BASED ON MINIMUM WAGE IN SÃO PAULO)

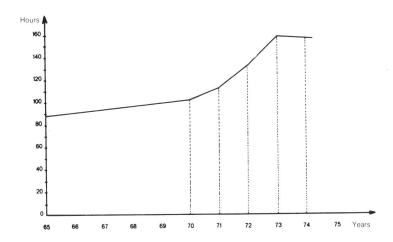

Source of data: DIEESE, in *Jornal da Tarde* newspaper, 30 April 1975.

Note: The minimum essential diet, per person, per month, as defined by law, is composed of the following
items:

13.2 lbs of meat   13.2 lbs of bread
13.2 pints of milk   1.32 lbs of coffee powder
9.9 lbs of black beans   90 bananas
6.6 lbs of rice   6.6 lbs of sugar
3.3 lbs of flour   1.65 lbs of lard
13.2 lbs of potatoes   1.65 lbs of butter
19.8 lbs of tomatoes

TABLE 12   CHANGES IN EMPLOYMENT AND INCOME
OF AVERAGE WORKING-CLASS FAMILY
IN CITY OF SÃO PAULO, 1958-69

	1958	1969
Number of members	4.5	4.9
Members employed	1.0	2.0
Monthly income (current prices)	cr$10.15	cr$512.10
Real monthly income (1958 prices)	cr$10.15	cr$9.20
Monthly wage of family head (current prices)	cr$8.54	cr$361.03
Real monthly wage of family head (1958 prices)	cr$8.54	cr$5.42

Source: DIEESE, 'Família assalariada; padrão e custo de vida', *op.cit.*, p.25.

TABLE 13   NON-AGRICULTURAL LABOUR FORCE:
WEEKLY HOURS OF WORK (SÃO PAULO)

	% of total of employed persons	
Number of hours of work per week	1968 (2nd quarter)	1972 (4th quarter)
Up to 14	1.6	1.0
From 15 to 39	14.8	11.3
From 40 to 49	59.4	59.5
50 and over	24.2	28.2
Total	*100.0*	*100.0*

Source: *PNAD 1968* and *1972*, in Singer P., 'A economia brasileira depois de 1964,' in *Debate e Crítica*, São Paulo, no. 4, November, 1974.

advantage does not mean however that São Paulo is exempt from the trend towards income concentration observed in the country as a whole in recent years.

The changing living standards of the typical working family in the city of São Paulo can be observed in two surveys carried out in 1958 and 1969 by DIEESE, the Inter-Trade Union Department of Statistics and Socio-Economic Studies. A comparison of the two surveys (see table 12) shows that over the intervening 11 years, the purchasing power of the wage of the head of the average family fell by 36.5%. To compensate for this loss, the family was compelled to send more of its members out to work. Even with more members working, however, the family's real income still fell by 9.4%. For lesser skilled workers, the deterioration in living standards was even greater, as can be seen from the fall in value of the minimum wage (see graphs 5 and 6).

Regular surveys carried out by DIEESE show that the period of work required to acquire the minimum essential diet has risen considerably in São Paulo over the last 10 years. As a result the number of hours worked by employees has increased, apparently to compensate for the fall in the real value of wages (see table 13). This trend can be illustrated by the fact that in 1972 in Greater São Paulo, the proportion of those who worked over 50 hours a week was 20.38% of those workers earning up to one minimum wage, and 26.54% of those earning between one and 2 minimum wages. In other words, the cost of climbing the wage ladder is determined by the extreme effort demanded of the work force.

The relationship between wage levels and number of hours worked is important for an understanding of the economic significance of the minimum wage. Insofar as it is insufficient to provide the basic needs of the working family,[39] the minimum wage represents the instrument by which the rapacious exploitation of the work force is encouraged and legitimised. Overtime, the employment of women both inside and outside the home, child labour — these are the expedients to which the working class family must resort to ensure its survival. The household budget is balanced because the labour power of more members of the family is put on the market and the length of the working day is extended. This increase of labour power placed at the disposal of capital further increases profits, given that the cost of maintaining the worker remains constant.

Moreover, the reduction of the minimum wage to a ridiculously low level leads not only to the gross exploitation of unskilled workers, but also to an undermining of skilled workers' wages. In the more dynamic and technologically advanced companies and sectors of the economy, the existence of a greater range of job categories gives rise to a greater range of wages. While the wages of less skilled workers are kept at a level close to the minimum allowed by law, the incomes of highly skilled workers in comparison reach somewhat higher levels.

Even so, labour productivity grows considerably faster than the average real wage in Greater São Paulo. In this way, productivity gains do not lead to wage increases for the workers as a whole, but constitute instead an additional source of capital accumulation for the firm.

The widening of working-class wage differentials does not contradict the process of income concentration, which is made possible by a growing surplus appropriated by a small minority, both as income from property (in the form of profits, interest and dividends), and in the form of income generated by labour. It is true that continued income concentration, which is characteristic of the expansion of the economy, does not affect all wage-earners equally. In 1972, over 50% of people with a healthy income of more than 10 minimum wages in Brazil were 'wage-earners'.[40] A good proportion of those who receive such high wages hold technical posts which in most cases do not involve directly productive activity. They have administrative,

---

39. According to surveys carried out by DIEESE, to comply with the standards laid down by the Constitution with respect to "the minimum remuneration required to satisfy, in a given country, the normal necessities of feeding, housing, clothing, hygiene and transport" (Decree Law no. 339), the minimum wage in 1975 should have been cr$1880.44: See *Opinião* newspaper no. 130, 2 May 1975, p.8.
40. P. Singer, *op.cit.*

technical-scientific or management jobs and the pattern of remuneration is much closer to that of capital ownership than of the productive process properly speaking.[41] The very growth in wages of the upper strata of employees is thus linked to the needs of the accumulation process. It is made possible only as long as average growth in wages is less than growth in production. The cost is the lowering of living standards of most workers.

One effect of the process of income concentration has been to stimulate the production of goods for consumption by the upper-income levels, thus encouraging the growth of the corresponding industrial sectors: the motor industry, the electrical and electronic goods industry, etc.

At the same time, consumer credit facilities have enabled some sectors of the population to participate in the durable and luxury consumer goods market, thus further stimulating these branches of industrial activity. The illusions and expectations created by advertising have, by influencing the way in which less well-off families spend their money, played an important role in expanding the market for the consumer goods manufacturers. Many people, in order to acquire possessions which symbolise prestige or success, have signed away their future earnings in the form of hire-purchase debts, or even sacrificed the satisfaction of their immediate basic needs: food, clothing, health and housing. Meanwhile the industrial sectors which supply goods for popular consumption have suffered accordingly, not only because of the new pattern of family spending, but principally through the absolute reduction in the purchasing power of large sectors of the population.

An illustration of this tendency can be seen in the changed pattern of consumption of wage-earners in São Paulo. Between 1958 and 1970 the consumption of working-class families became more diversified, with the number of products purchased rising from 155 to 184. The pattern of spending also changed, with a relative drop in expenditure on food, clothing, items of personal hygiene and domestic cleaning, and an increase in other items such as transport, household goods, education, culture, recreation and tobacco.

The fall in expenditure on food — which accounted for over 45% of total outlay in 1958, but only 39% in 1970[42] — is usually interpreted as an

41. According to a recent survey, the growth-rate of the average wage between 1966 and 1969 in the country's manufacturing industry was 5.5% for wage-earners linked to 'administration' and 3.3% for those linked to 'production' (Relatório IPEA no.26). It should be noted that the report refers exclusively to the *growth rates* of average wages, and not to their respective *absolute* levels. A comparison of the absolute figures would show the existence of wage differentials of over 10,000%.

42. Or 64.3% and 51% in 1970, if housing costs are excluded (see table 14).

TABLE 14   MODIFICATIONS IN WORKING-CLASS CONSUMPTION
IN SÃO PAULO, 1958 AND 1970

Item of expenditure	% of total family budget excluding housing costs* 1958	1970
Food	64.3	51.0
Clothing	14.3	10.6
Health	5.7	4.7
Domestic cleaning	4.3	2.2
Household goods	4.3	8.5
Transport	2.9	11.5
Personal hygiene	2.1	1.6
Education and culture	1.4	4.6
Recreation and tobacco	0.7	5.3
Total	*100.0*	*100.0*

Source: DIEESE, 'Familia assalarida: padrão e custo de vida', *op.cit.*

*Housing costs represented 30% of the total budget in 1958 and 23.5% in 1970. However, the 1958 sample only included families living in rented accommodation. As two-thirds of working-class families in São Paulo own their own house, housing expenses were over-estimated in the 1958 survey. In the above table, the figures have been re-calculated to remove the distortion produced in the remaining items by this error.

indication of an improved standard of living. Taking into consideration the falling income of the families in question over the same period, however, the only possible conclusion is that *per capita* food consumption fell, "indicating a deterioration in the nutrition standards of the working population".[43]

Over the same period, transport costs rose considerably for all income levels included in the survey. However, while for the lower income level this increase can be basically attributed to greater travelling distances and an increased use of public transport, 70.6% of transport costs of the upper income level in 1970 was accounted for by the purchase of vehicles and petrol. There can be no doubt that the car, which began to be produced in the country on a large scale precisely in the period under study, affected consumption patterns of higher-income wage-earners. The increase in expenditure on household goods is a direct reflection of the incorporation of electrical and electronic goods into the wage-earners' way of life. In both the

43.   DIEESE, 'Família assalariada: padrão e custo de vida,' *op.cit.*

lower and the middle income levels, these products accounted for around 60% of expenditure on household goods in 1970. Television alone represented 42% of spending in this category for the lower income level, and 29.1% for the middle income level. As regards expenditure on recreation and tobacco, 94% went on cigarettes in all income levels in 1970. The enormous increase which took place could have been due both to the rise in cigarette prices and the increased popularity of smoking. As regards expenditure on education and culture, most went on school expenses.

Modifications in the living standards of wage-earners in São Paulo can be explained by two sets of factors: first, changes in the economic sphere demanding a greater outlay on transport and education by the working family; and second, the appearance of 'new products' which, depending on the family's standard of living, are eventually transformed into necessitities: the role played by the car for the upper income level is played by the television for the middle and lower income levels.

Obviously when new needs are introduced into workers' patterns of consumption, they raise the subsistence costs of the working family. A corresponding increase in wages ought therefore to be expected. At the same time, if the new products are to be manufactured, someone has to be able to buy them and this implies an increase in the income at the disposal of the population. As has been seen, the development model put into operation in recent years has involved increases in wage differentials, creating a level of higher income for technical and skilled workers. However, for most of the working class the new standards of living have meant the sacrifice of such essentials as food, medical care, hygiene and clothing. Since the real income of a typical wage-earning family in São Paulo fell by 9.4% between 1958 and 1969, the participation of the working class in the new consumer opportunities made available by the market has been possible only through a reduction in their consumption of food, clothes, medicines and medical services, and products of personal hygiene and domestic cleaning.

These conditions tend to be self-perpetuating given that the new patterns of consumption strengthen the profitability of the more modern industrial sectors. These are the sectors which create the new needs, as much by marketing their new products as by their demands for a skilled labour force. However, for these conditions to continue, they demand an even greater lowering of the living standards of certain sectors of the population. For skilled workers to be better paid, while the level of average earnings remains constant, the real wages of the less skilled have to be reduced. If the nutrition and health standards of the working class are to be reduced without harming production, either companies' labour needs must be diminished or the length of productive activity of individual workers must be shortened. One way or another, it is a question of continually selecting the more able and excluding the rest from the opportunity of a job and an income. This is only possible while the number of workers available is greater than that needed by the employers, and while the ability of the working class as a whole to demand better wages is held in check.

4
Poor, poorer and poorest

The extreme differences in the way people live in Greater São Paulo are determined by how much they earn and the way in which they are paid. These factors are in turn the result of the different job opportunities open to the various sectors of the population. As the urban-industrial economy develops, the organisation of the production of goods and services becomes more complex, leading to the emergence of new and different forms of work. Furthermore, the changes in the organisation of production, the increasing use of more efficient machines and equipment and the higher level of skills of the workers themselves, mean that labour productivity rises, with the result that employers need relatively less labour. The outcome of these trends is that both job opportunities and income levels become more varied for the different sectors which make up the population.

In spite of the growing demand for certain categories of workers, employment opportunities in general have not necessarily kept pace with population growth. The findings of the National Household Sample Survey indicate that the degree of participation in the work force — in other words the proportion of the population which is either working or looking for work — is decreasing in Greater São Paulo. In the last quarter of 1971, the work force was made up of 3.5 million people or 53.8% of all the 6.5 million inhabitants of the city aged 10 years or more. (Though many children under 10 years can be found working, this is the lowest age usually included in official employment statistics.) A year later, in the last quarter of 1972, the work force numbered 3.6 million of a total 6.8 million residents of 10 years or more, a figure which represents a proportion of 52.4%.

As far as job opportunities are concerned, the situation depends on whether the worker is skilled or unskilled. Most firms in Greater São Paulo employ a work force which does not require a lengthy apprenticeship, only a short period of training. In 1972-3, for example, of the 735,000 employees of the Capital's industrial sector, only 18% were skilled.[44]

The fact that there are more workers than are needed for production enables employers to establish preferences for certain categories of workers which are not based simply on the skill required for the job. Instead such characteristics as sex, age, origin, skin colour, and so on, assume importance in job selection. The preferences for men rather than women, younger people rather than older, migrants rather than non-migrants, whites rather than blacks, can be the result as much of economic factors as of social prejudice. On the other hand the discrimination against certain categories of workers illustrates how prejudice can be used for economic ends, as in the case, for example, of the lower wages paid to women and children for doing the same work as adult men. Alternatively, economic discrimination can give rise to social discrimination, for example when employees are worked to exhaustion and then replaced by younger workers, thus creating a category of 'old' workers which has little direct relationship to their biological age. In this way, social and economic discrimination reinforce one another, differentiating between workers and excluding certain groups from the labour market.

In Greater São Paulo between 1971 and 1972, the number of economically active men as a proportion of all males aged 10 years and over dropped from 74.9% to 73.6%. For women, the proportion similarly fell from 33.2% to 31.6%.[45] This reduction is the result of two processes: on the one hand, young people are entering the work force later, due to a longer period spent at school at least for certain groups, coupled with a decreasing demand for child labour; and on the other, workers considered to be old are being replaced by younger workers, leading to withdrawal from the work force at an earlier age.

An analysis of the unemployment figures shows that, for people over 10 years old, the proportion of the male work force which is unemployed is no less than 12.9%. For women this figure is 12.0%.[46] However, since the

44. *Relatório SENAI, 1973*, São Paulo, 1974.

45. See *PNAD — Regiões Metropolitanas, 4.° Trimestre, 1971-72*, Rio de Janeiro, IBGE, no date.

46. See table 15. 'Unemployed' includes not only people with no occupation who are seeking jobs, but also those included in the National Household Sample Survey (PNAD) category of 'others' who are able to work. The percentages given in the text are reached by adding the figures for 'those with no occupation' with 'others' in the National Household Sample Survey tables.

TABLE 15 THE WORK FORCE,
UNEMPLOYMENT AND INACTIVITY BY SEX AND AGE
IN GREATER SÃO PAULO IN 1972

Age groups	% of total population in work force		Unemployed as % of work force*		% of 'others' in total population**	
	Men	Women	Men	Women	Men	Women
10 — 14	9.4	7.7	12.0	6.6	10.8	7.7
15 — 19	70.0	49.5	8.6	7.2	6.5	2.9
20 — 24	91.0	51.0	4.7	4.6	2.3	1.0
25 — 29	96.8	38.7	2.5	1.4	1.4	1.1
30 — 39	94.8	34.2	1.3	2.4	1.6	0.6
40 — 49	92.6	30.6	0.7	0.5	3.9	0.4
50 — 59	74.9	20.2	0.6	0.3	23.3	2.9
60 — 69	46.0	10.3	0.4	—	43.0	4.4
70 plus	16.1	1.5	—	—	64.1	18.3
Total	*73.6*	*31.6*	*3.0*	*4.0*	*8.4*	*2.9*
14 years or more	*84.4*	*35.3*				

Source: *PNAD, Regiões Metropolitanas. 4° trimestre, 1971-1972*, Rio de Janeiro, IBGE, no date, p.233.
*Includes unemployed who have taken measures to find work in the last 2 months, and those seeking work for the first time.
**'Others' are persons outside the work force who are neither occupied in domestic tasks, nor go to school, nor are incapable of working.

TABLE 16 PERCENTAGE OF WOMEN WHO ARE HEADS OF FAMILIES,
WIVES, OR WHO WORK IN THE HOME,
IN GREATER SÃO PAULO, 1972.

Age Groups	Family Heads	Wives	Work in Home
15 — 19	0.2	8.7	21.2
20 — 24	2.1	39.5	42.4
25 — 29	3.9	65.6	38.0
30 — 39	6.0	79.5	63.4
40 — 49	12.6	76.0	66.8
50 — 59	19.5	64.0	80.0
60 — 69	23.6	43.4	81.4
70 plus	25.3	15.0	69.5

Source: *PNAD, op.cit.*, pp.228-33.

proportion of women who work outside the home is known to be small compared with men, we would suggest that the figure for female unemployment obscures another phenomenon. This is the 'hidden' unemployment, so-called because it does not appear in the statistics, of the enormous number of women who neither have jobs nor are studying, but who for survey purposes are designated as working in the home. The fact is that to be 'unemployed' appears to be a male prerogative in our society. A woman who has no paid work can always find something to do at home and thus does not declare herself unemployed. Most women who work outside the home are between 20 and 24 years old, after this age the number of women who work outside the home decreases steadily.

Moving from younger to older groups, the proportion of those employed begins to fall off from 30 years old onwards for women and after 50 years old for men. The statistics reveal a selectivity in the use of labour in terms of the age at which workers are excluded from employment. This selectivity occurs because the male work force is sufficiently numerous as to render a large proportion of the female work force unnecesary from the age of 30 years and onwards, and to enable male workers over 50 years of age to be replaced by younger workers. In this respect it is significant that while the proportion of unemployed men aged 40-49 years is only 4.7%, this figure leaps upwards in the older age-groups; between 50 and 59 years it is 19.4%, between 60 and 69 years it rises to 47.9%, and over 70 years it is 80.0%.

A cycle of productive life has thus been created which allows employers to abuse their employees by excluding tired workers from the labour market. Because of the size of the available work force, older workers are decreed incapable of work and are pushed out of their jobs. Of course many of them are prematurely categorised as 'old' since they are still in full possession of both their physical and mental capabilities.

It is a mistake to assume that, with advancing age, people withdraw from a working life because they want to retire and can afford to give up their jobs. On the contrary, it is common knowledge that during their working life most workers cannot manage to save up enough for their old age. It is also well known that, for the majority, pensions, when they exist at all, are not even enough to meet essential living expenses. In addition, there is the question of those who are working without cards, a problem which becomes more serious the older the age-group considered. Between the ages of 15 and 39 years, the proportion of male employees with valid work cards is above 70% of the total. In the 40-49 years age-group, this proportion drops to 63%, from 50-59 years it is 50%, at 60 years it is 40% and at 70 years it is only 20%.

Discrimination against women workers is even worse. The age-group with the highest proportion of properly registered workers is 20-24 years with 64%; thereafter the proportion decreases steadily. For those aged between 25 and 29 years it is 56%, and between 30 and 39 years it is 48%. For older women it falls even more steeply with the result that in the 60-69 years age-group, only 16% have valid work cards. This situation is to a great extent explained by the large number of women who work in domestic service — over a quarter of the female work force in Greater São Paulo. Apart from the 35% of women workers who have jobs classified as the 'provision of services', women also work in the 'manufacturing industry' (29%), 'social service' (13%), and 'wholesale and retail trade' (9%). The division of the male labour force between the different sectors is as follows: 40% in the 'manufacturing industry', 14% in the 'wholesale and retail trade', 14% in the 'provision of services', 7% in the 'building industry' and 7% in 'transport, communication and warehousing' (see table 17).

TABLE 17 SECTORS OF ECONOMIC ACTIVITY, BY SEX,
IN GREATER SÃO PAULO, 1972
(IN PERCENTAGES)

Sector of activity	*Totals*	Men	Women
Primary sector	*1.9*	*2.2*	*1.1*
Agriculture	1.5	1.7	1.1
Mineral extraction	0.4	0.5	0.1
Secondary sector	*42.1*	*47.4*	*29.7*
Manufacturing industry	36.4	39.6	29.0
Building industry	5.0	6.9	0.4
Industrial work of public utility	0.7	0.9	0.3
Tertiary sector	*56.0*	*50.4*	*69.2*
Wholesale and retail trade	12.8	14.3	9.4
Provision of services	20.3	14.0	34.8*
Transport and communications, warehousing	5.0	6.7	1.1
Liberal professions	2.3	2.4	2.8
Social services	6.1	3.1	13.1
Public administration	4.2	4.7	3.0
Others	5.1	5.2	5.0
Total	*100.0*	*100.0*	*100.0*

Source: *PNAD, op.cit.*, p.240.
*Of whom 75.3% are domestic servants, ie 26.2% of the total female work force.

Discrimination against the employment of older people has been increasing in recent decades. This can be seen from the fact that in the state of São Paulo, the percentage of men over 45 years old with jobs fell from 88% in 1940 to 84% in 1950 and to 71% in 1970.[47] Discrimination against women dates back even further. In the past it was unusual for women to have paid employment other than working on the land or doing various kinds of handicraft which could be practised at home. With the onset of industrialisation women are gradually gaining a place in the labour market, particularly in the tertiary sector occupations: domestic service, nursing, primary school teaching, office work etc.

On the other hand, as women start gaining employment in certain occupations, these jobs are labelled as 'female', with the result that men begin to withdraw from them. An obvious example is primary school teaching, which in the past was a field dominated by men, but which nowadays has become reserved almost exclusively for women. Other fields such as librarianship, social services, and a number of auxiliary roles in medicine are showing the same trend. It is as if men cannot withstand the competition from women and leave the field as soon as a certain number of women move into it. In reality, however, this 'inability to compete' is due to the lower wages paid to women.

Statistics on standards of education also reveal discrimination. Working women tend to have a higher degree of schooling than working men: 21% finish the first 4-year cycle of secondary school, as against 19% of men; 14% complete the second cycle, as opposed to 8% of men; and 9% have completed university courses, compared with only 7% of men. However, this does not mean that women as a whole have a higher standard of education than men. On the contrary, the proportion of illiterates is greater among women (13%) than among men (8%), though smaller among working women (6%), compared with working men (7%). These figures suggest that to a certain extent women manage to surmount the barriers of the labour market when they can show a higher level of schooling than men. In jobs requiring higher educational qualifications and in which, moreover, pay is on average better, the tendency is to employ relatively more women. However, the pay for women in these occupations is notably less than for men. This is the case, for example, in 'administration' in which the median female wage is from 2 to 3 minimum wages, while for men it is from 3 to 5. The same situation exists in 'technical, scientific, and artistic' occupations,

47.   Spindel C.R., *Disponibilidade e Aproveitamento dos Recursos Humanos do Estado de São Paulo e da Região Metropolitana*, CEBRAP, São Paulo, 1973 (Cadernos CEBRAP no.15).

TABLE 18 EDUCATIONAL LEVEL, BY SEX,
OF PERSONS 10 YEARS OF AGE OR MORE,
WHETHER WORKING OR NOT,
IN GREATER SÃO PAULO, 1972

Educational Level	Men			Women		
	Total	Working*	Not working	*Total*	Working*	Not working
Illiterate	*7.6*	6.5	5.4	*13.1*	5.7	7.0
Primary school	*58.5*	59.5	64.5	*57.5*	50.9	51.7
Secondary school						
1st cycle	*20.6*	18.9	21.1	*18.5*	20.9	27.2
2nd cycle	*7.3*	8.1	4.9	*7.8*	13.9	9.8
University	*6.0*	7.0	4.1	*3.1*	8.6	4.3
Total	*100.0*	*100.0*	*100.0*	*100.0*	*100.0*	*100.0*

Source: *PNAD, op.cit.,* p.264.
*Only those receiving cash wages.

TABLE 19 EDUCATIONAL LEVEL OF WOMEN BY AGE,
IN GREATER SÃO PAULO, 1972

Age groups	*Total*	Literate	Primary school	Others
10 — 14	*477,225*	98.5%	58.0%	40.5%
15 — 19	*462,984*	96.8%	44.0%	52.8%
20 — 24	*452,505*	95.0%	55.8%	39.2%
25 — 29	*383,443*	92.3%	61.7%	30.6%
30 — 39	*637,104*	88.6%	65.9%	22.7%
40 — 49	*471,282*	81.0%	65.8%	15.2%
50 — 59	*294,202*	69.1%	57.0%	12.1%
60 — 69	*175,032*	60.6%	45.4%	15.2%
70 plus	*99,198*	49.7%	41.9%	7.8%
Total	*3,452,975*	*87.2%*	*57.7%*	*29.5%*
Women in work force	1,087,202	92.2%	55.1%	37.1%
Men in work force	2,486,966	93.1%	59.5%	33.6%

Source: *PNAD, op.cit.,* pp.238 and 276-80.

TABLE 20 OCCUPATIONAL GROUPS AND WAGES
(IN TERMS OF MINIMUM WAGE), BY SEX,
IN GREATER SÃO PAULO, 1972

Occupation	Men	Median wage*	Women	Median wage*	Total	Median wage*
Administration	18.6	3—5	27.5	2—3	21.2	2—3
Technical, scientific and artistic	6.3	5—7	12.1	2—3	8.0	3—5
Farming, vegetable and animal extraction	1.2	0.5—1	0.2	0.25—0.5	0.9	0.5—1
Mineral extraction	0.2	1—2	——	——	0.1	1—2
Manufacturing and building industry	35.7	1—2	23.8	1—2	32.3	1—2
Trade and allied activities	8.0	1—2	5.5	1—2	7.3	1—2
Transport and communications	6.6	2—3	1.0	1—2	4.9	2—3
Provision of services	1.9	1—2	20.0	0.5—1	7.2	0.5—1
Others	21.5	1—2	9.9	1—2	18.1	1—2
Total/average	*100.0*	*2—3*	*100.0*	*1—2*	*100.0*	*1—2*

Source: *PNAD, op.cit.,* p.267.
*In numbers of minimum wages.

in which women earn from 2 to 3 minimum wages, while men get from 5 to 7 (see table 20). To summarise, in occupations which require a higher standard of education, employers prefer to take on women because, due to the non-implementation of legislation guaranteeing equal pay for both sexes, they can pay them less than they pay men. On the other hand, with regard to low-paid jobs in which education is not an important requirement and wages are near the minimum, the preference for male labour predominates (with the exception of domestic service, which is traditionally a woman's job).

As far as younger workers are concerned, the effects of greater education should be emphasised. The extension of schooling affects a considerable proportion of the working classes at least where elementary schooling is concerned. Consequently, the younger generation has a higher standard of education than the older. However, this is not the whole of the question. It is necessary to clarify whether the extension of schooling opens up more opportunities for social improvement for poorer people or whether, given the new requirements of the labour market, it merely reinforces existing differences.

In urban-industrial societies, the education system is significant for the job opportunities it opens up. The child or young person who either cannot attend school or who is obliged to leave it prematurely will in the future have fewer opportunities of access to a number of occupations which demand a certain standard of education. The future skilled employee is to a great extent determined by his schooling.

Despite the increasing number of children and young people who attend school in São Paulo, there are still many who are obliged to end their studies prematurely. There are statistics which indicate a relative deterioration at the elementary level in Greater São Paulo: in 1966, 10% of children aged 7 to 14 were not at school, but by 1971 this proportion had risen to 20%.[48] Many are forced to leave school early because of the socio-economic situation of their families. In the great majority of cases, they are children and young people who are obliged to go to work at an early age: 9.4% of boys and 7.7% of girls of 10 to 14 years of age who live in Greater São Paulo go to work (see table 15). These figures reveal a process of education interrupted in mid-course.

Going out to work so early is socially detrimental in two ways: it means both an inadequate education (in that the young person ends up with only a partial schooling), and a job which is very unlikely to provide any skilled training. The kind of work generally available to minors does not demand much skill or knowledge. Whether working in the street, in the market, or in someone's home, as a seller, porter, 'watchman' or domestic servant, or as an errand boy in an office or a labourer in a factory, their tasks do not require previously-learned techniques. Training is not necessary for such routines. Neither do such jobs provide training in a skill which might give the young workers the future chance of better-paid employment.

Going out to work at an early age is but one of the factors that limits the opportunities for improvement in the future. Another and perhaps more crucial factor which leads to similar restrictions is 'inactivity': about 14% of boys and 17% of girls from 10 to 14 years old neither study nor work. These

48. *Região Metropolitana de São Paulo: Diagnóstico 1975. Desenvolvimento Sócio-Econômico: Educação, op.cit.* The same report also reveals that between 1971 and 1973, the average annual level of absenteeism in the first four years of secondary school was 12%; in 1970 it was 7.5% and in 1972, 10%. According to *Diagnóstico 1975: Promoção Social, ibid.,* 98% of children in the Metropolitan Region do not have access to play facilities and only 1% regularly go to nurseries or supervised playgrounds. For every 100 children who entered the first year of primary school in 1967, only 67 passed straight through to the fourth year in 1970 without repeating classes or dropping out; similarly, in secondary schools in the same period, of every 100 in the first year, only 72 passed directly to the fourth year four years later.

girls soon get into the routine of doing household chores.[49] In the next age-group, from 15 to 19 years of age, the proportion at work is greater and the number attending school correspondingly declines. Even so, it is worth noting that 16.3% of boys and 12.3% of girls in this age-group have no occupation. Moreover, 21.2% of girls in this age-group spend their time working in the home, although only 8.9% of them are married or in charge of families. In other words, from an early age, domestic service helps to disguise unemployment (see tables 15 and 16).

Both young people who work and those who neither work nor study soon find themselves facing a future devoid of opportunities for social and economic improvement. There is no evidence to suggest that this bleak prospect is due to the lack of individual abilities. On the contrary, the root of the problem is social and stems from their families' material and cultural deprivation.

Although the development of the urban-industrial economy in Greater São Paulo has involved modification of labour skills with a consequent diversification of jobs, it is principally parental 'inheritance' which decides the range of socio-economic opportunities available to workers and determines where they will end up in the occupational hierarchy. The remodelling of the economy and of society can be said to reflect the differences between social groups. Thus, working-class children are destined to a rudimentary form of education, which provides an early training for work, and in which both social and cultural formation and practical training are designed,to guide them towards their destination in the least skilled jobs.

The diversification of the economy also leads to the creation of specialised jobs. However, the extent of this phenomenon should not be exaggerated. Unskilled labour still predominates and is the result of methods of production which depend overwhelmingly on repetitive gestures, concentrated attention and considerable physical effort. On the other hand, for the children of middle-class parents, new technical and administrative occupations often requiring a university education are created in both the public and the private sector. While 'clean' jobs — in the so-called liberal professions — are most people's preference, 'dirty' work — manual labour — is considered inferior. The difference between the two kinds of work depends on access to certain areas of study, which itself is a question of class. Not only do few working-class children make it to secondary school — and those who do are usually the children of supervisors or skilled workers —

49.   The proportion of those who cannot actually work is 0.8% for males and 0.6% for females, according to the National Household Sample Survey (PNAD).

TABLE 21 DISTRIBUTION OF ECONOMICALLY ACTIVE SECTOR
OF BRAZILIAN POPULATION, BY COLOUR,
IN 1950 (IN PERCENTAGES)

Colour	Employees	Employers	Self-employed	Family member	Undeclared
Whites	48.75	5.11	28.30	17.63	0.18
Mulattos	44.90	1.84	34.22	18.80	0.19
Blacks	60.91	0.95	24.51	13.40	0.16
Orientals	23.35	10.29	31.79	34.35	0.25

Source: *Recenseamento Geral do Brasil*, IBGE, 1950

but most of those who do get there opt for technical training courses. Middle-class children have access to more academic courses, which give them a good chance of entering higher education, while of the children of poorer sectors of the population, the few who get this far are channelled into training courses.[50] For the individual the opportunities created by the development of São Paulo can in certain cases lead to improved living standards. However, from the point of view of the community as a whole, the economic growth of the city has involved the perpetuation of existing inequalities.

The existence of racial discrimination can be taken as an indication that the perpetuation of inequalities in São Paulo has little to do with the 'free competition of the market' which, in capitalist ideology, is the expression of the 'natural' character of the social hierarchy.[51] A look at some statistics about the position of different ethnic groups in the labour market is illuminating. As illustrated by the figures for colour and occupation in the whole of Brazil in 1950 (see table 21),[52] 5.1% of whites were classified as employers, 28.3% as self-employed and 48.8% as employees. On the other hand, while 60.9% of blacks were employees and 24.5% self-employed, less than 1% were employers. The situation for mulattos (the offspring of black and white parentage) was somewhat different—proportionally few of them

50. Kowarick L. and Camargo C.P.F., *Problemas Quantitativos e Qualitativos da Educação no Estado de São Paulo*, CEBRAP, São Paulo, 1971, p.21 (mimeo).
51. The following observations have been taken in a condensed form from Ianni O., *Negritude e Cidadania*, São Paulo, 1975 (unpublished).
52. 1950 is the last year for which census data are available on the colour of the Brazilian population. In the 1960 census, respondents were asked to give their colour but the answers were not analysed. In 1970, this question was not even asked.

TABLE 22 DISTRIBUTION OF ECONOMICALLY ACTIVE SECTOR
OF POPULATION OF SÃO PAULO STATE, 1950*
(IN PERCENTAGES)

Type of occupation

Colour	Employee	Employer	Self-employed	Family member
Whites	65.2	5.2	16.3	13.4
Mulattos	75.5	1.3	11.4	11.8
Blacks	79.4	0.9	9.1	10.6
Orientals	23.3	10.1	31.7	34.8
Total	*65.7*	*4.8*	*15.9*	*13.6*

Source: *VI Recenseamento Geral do Brasil — 1950 — Série Regional, vol. XXV — tomo I, Estado de São Paulo,* Rio de Janeiro, IBGE Graphical Service, 1954, p.30.
*Responses not specifying type of occupation have been omitted.

TABLE 23 DISTRIBUTION OF MEN AND WOMEN
OF 10 YEARS AND OVER, BY TYPE OF
OCCUPATION AND BY COLOUR,
IN MUNICIPALITY OF SÃO PAULO, IN 1940
(IN PERCENTAGES)

Type of occupation	Whites	Blacks	Mulattos	Orientals	*Total*
Employers	3.6	0.3	0.6	7.1	*3.4*
Employees	77.6	85.6	84.2	47.8	*76.9*
Self-employed	17.6	11.6	12.3	32.5	*17.4*
Family member	1.1	0.5	0.4	11.7	*1.2*
Unknown	1.0	2.0	2.5	0.9	*1.1*
Total	*100.0*	*100.0*	*100.0*	*100.0*	*100.0*

Source: *Recenseamento Geral do Brasil,* IBGE, 1940, in Fernandes F., *A Integração do Negro na Sociedade de Classes,* São Paulo, Dominus and EDUSP, 1965, vol. 2, p.102.

were employers (1.8%), but more of them (34.2%) were self-employed.[53] The occupational structure in the state of São Paulo is, however, somewhat different, as table 22 shows. In 1950 a higher proportion of blacks and mulattos was numbered among employees and a lesser proportion among employers, while the incidence of white employers and employees was greater.

Statistics for the occupational status of blacks and mulattos in the city of São Paulo are not available for 1950 but only for 1940. In that year, blacks comprised only 4.79% of the population of the municipality of São Paulo, and mulattos 3.40%. Whites accounted for 90.72% and people of oriental descent for 1.06%. According to table 23, most blacks worked as employees (85.6%), only 0.3% were employers and 11.6% self-employed. The pattern for mulattos was slightly different, with 0.6% as employers and 12.3% working for themselves. In contrast, 3.6% of whites were employers, 17.6% worked for themselves, and 77.6% were employees. Among orientals, there was a high proportion of employers (7.1%) and self-employed (32.5%).

There are no census data on the ethnic composition of the population of São Paulo (whether the municipality or the Metropolitan Region) for 1960 and 1970. We know, however, that the population of the municipality and the Metropolitan Region has grown considerably — much faster than its rate of natural growth. From 1960 to 1970, the population of the municipality grew 4.54% a year. This rate includes a natural growth rate (net number of births minus deaths) of some 2.13% a year, and growth due to migration of around 2.85% a year. In the same period, the annual rates of growth in the Metropolitan Region were 5.50% overall, 2.36% in natural growth and 3.76% in growth due to migration (see table 3). There are indications that growth due to migration which took place in both areas included a large number of blacks and mulattos. It is worth mentioning in passing that until 1956 the majority of migrants were mulattos rather than whites or blacks. From 1957 whites became the largest single group. This does not, however, mean that blacks and mulattos stopped arriving in São Paulo in large numbers.[54] In 1970, as table 24 shows, they still accounted for a considerable proportion of all migrants. Another indication of the proportional increase of blacks and mulattos in São Paulo can be seen in the statistics on the ethnic distribution of live-born children in the municipality of São Paulo in 1961. In that year, black and mulatto children accounted for

53. The statistics quoted here in the text and in tables 21 and 22 have been taken from Fernandes F., *O Negro no Mundo dos Brancos,* São Paulo, DIFEL, pp.56-61.

54. Jordão Netto A., *Aspectos Econômicos e Sociais das Migrações Internas para o Estado de São Paulo,* São Paulo, 1973, pp.111-22 (mimeo).

TABLE 24 DISTRIBUTION OF MIGRANTS, BY COLOUR,
IN CITY OF SÃO PAULO, 1970

Colour	Number	%
White	163	50.93
Mulatto	101	31.56
Black	65	17.50
Total	*320*	*100.0*

Source: Jordão Netto, A., *op.cit.*, p.109.

13.70% of all births. We may therefore conclude that the black and mulatto population in São Paulo grew in the years 1950-60.

In 1950, blacks and mulattos totalled 10.22% of the population surveyed in the municipality of São Paulo.[55] According to a survey carried out in 1967, the 'marginal' population of Greater São Paulo included about 39% of blacks and mulattos at that time (see table 25).[56] We may therefore assume that blacks and mulattos in the city of São Paulo and its metropolitan area continue to live in adverse socio-economic and political circumstances. Relatively speaking, among blacks and mulattos there are more unemployed, illiterate, marginalised, impoverished and so on, a state of affairs that is confirmed by studies in this area. A survey carried out on the social marginalisation of minors in the area of São Paulo shows that blacks and mulattos are in high proportion to whites. According to a 1971 survey they make up 42.35% of all minors in care or detention.[57] This means that the proportion of black and mulatto children who are in care or detention is even higher that the proportion of blacks and mulattos among the 'marginal' population of Greater São Paulo, which according to table 25 is 39%.

In both the city and the Metropolitan Region of São Paulo, blacks and mulattos are principally employed in industry, commerce, transport, urban services and so on. A small number of them are lower middle class, but practically none are in the upper middle class. Moreover, within the working class itself, blacks and mulattos are generally at the bottom. The few who are in occupations of greater prestige usually have some occupation in the public eye, such as music or football. Often, however, they can only

55. Fernandes F., *A Integração do Negro na Sociedade de Classes*, op.cit., vol. 2, p.101, table 3.
56. *Levantamento Sócio-Econômico das Populacões Marginais — Região de São Paulo*, São Paulo, Fundação Plano de Amparo Social, 1969.
57. CEBRAP, *A Criança, o Adolescente e a Cidade, Semana de Estudos de Problemas dos Menores*, São Paulo, 1973, p.279.

TABLE 25   COMPOSITION OF POPULATION
ACCORDING TO COLOUR, 1967
(IN PERCENTAGES)

Colour	São Paulo Metropolitan Region	State of São Paulo
Whites	60.8	86.0
Blacks	8.3	8.0
Mulattos	30.7	3.0
Orientals	0.2	3.0
Total	*100.0*	*100.0*

Source: *Fundação Plano de Amparo Social, Levantamento Sócio-Econômico das Populações Marginais—Região de São Paulo*, São Paulo, 1969, p.95.

escape from heavy manual labour by taking jobs of lesser social standing, such as the civil or military police, selling odds and ends in the street, looking after parked cars and so on.

Discrimination against blacks not only bars their way to many jobs that are better-paid or of greater social standing, but also increases the likelihood of unemployment. None of this, however, bears any relation to their individual abilities or character. It is rather a question of social conditions which perpetuate the prejudice against blacks which dates back to the days of slavery. Ever since slavery was abolished, differences have existed between white workers and descendants of former slaves. On the other hand, immigrants and their descendants have since their arrival enjoyed better opportunities. Immigrants were given a minimum of protection and assistance, while former slaves were simply deprived of opportunities. Moreover, Italian, Spanish, German and other immigrants soon formed a system of self-help and assistance among themselves. Though this system obviously did not extend to all immigrants and their descendants, it did facilitate their assimilation and access to jobs, while blacks and mulattos were relegated to the sidelines. It was only with the new waves of industrialisation and urbanisation in the 1920s and 1930s that blacks and mulattos began to meet new opportunities in employment. Moreover, with the expansion of industry, transport, commerce and services after 1940, they began to participate in larger numbers in the wage-earning sector of the city and the Metropolitan Region.[58]

58.   Bastide R. and Fernandes F., *Brancos e Negros em São Paulo*, 2nd edition, São Paulo. Companhia Editora Nacional, 1959; Fernandes F., *A Integração do Negro na Sociedade de Classes*, op.cit.

To summarise, two main trends can be observed in race relations in São Paulo. In the first place, the expansion and growing complexity of urban-industrial society has opened up and diversified the labour market. Under these conditions, blacks and mulattos find new opportunities in jobs and training. On the other hand, in the competition for jobs in industry, commerce, transport and so on, racial prejudice puts blacks and mulattos at a disadvantage. They either remain unemployed or else work in jobs which are economically and socially inferior. Given the choice between a black, a mulatto and a white, the white employer tends to select the white, whether in the factory, the shop, the office, or in any other work. On the frequent occasions when the supply of labour exceeds demand, discrimination tends to increase. For this reason blacks and mulattos generally end up in the worst-paid jobs carrying the least social prestige.

Under such conditions, a culture based on ethnic and racial differences is preserved. Moreover, on the ideological plane, racial prejudice is associated with the process of economic marginalisation. The lowly economic position shared by blacks and mulattos with other sectors of the population means that they are all victims of the same social discrimination. Thus blacks and mulattos from Greater São Paulo are given the same perjorative nickname of 'Bahian' as migrants from Bahia and the North-East in general.

The process by which inequalities in São Paulo society are perpetuated affects all workers, but some sectors of them more than others. Juveniles, women, old people and blacks are more radically excluded from the chance of a job and a wage. However, this is not a question of individual problems. Reinforcing differences within the working class enables a more systematic exploitation of the work force. Moreover, in a situation where too many workers are chasing too few jobs, it facilitates the practice of working employees to exhaustion and then replacing them at low cost.

5

The struggle for participation

There was a time when most of the problems affecting the people of São Paulo were solved in the context of local government. Until the 18th century, government was in the hands of an elected council and, at special times, an assembly of 'good men and true' with full powers to resolve problems arising over "defence, relations with the Indians, ecclesiastical administration, control of prices and of commodities, public works and town services".[59]

Political power in the municipal councils of colonial times was a direct reflection of economic power in the local society. The 'good men and true' who elected the council representatives and made up the extraordinary assemblies were Christian property-owners. Political participation was not allowed to Jews, foreigners, artisans, rural workers, or "speaking generally, common people".[60]

Since then the franchise has gradually been extended. During the time of the Brazilian Empire (1822-89) it was extended to the wealthier sectors of society. Later, during the Republic, the franchise was granted to increasing sectors of the ordinary people. However, at the same time, the political system became more complicated. Municipal autonomy gradually gave way to the encroaching authority of central government. The powers of the bodies of popular representation diminished as a result of the expanding sphere of activity of the executive. These factors culminated in the current situation when everything, or almost everything, that happens in the city is beyond the control of its inhabitants.

59. Morse R.M., *Formação Histórica de São Paulo*, São Paulo, Difusão Européia do Livro, 1970, pp.30-3.
60. *Ibid.*, p.31.

The gap between elected representation and administrative power continued to widen as much at the municipal as at the state and federal government levels. This was due in part to the transference of decision-making powers in a number of areas, from the legislative to the executive, and was justified on grounds of greater efficiency.

The real reason for this transference is, however, to be found in the changing locus of power. The administration was in fact being removed from the influence of pressures and counter-pressures which typify democratic societies, but which are dismissed in Brazil as 'demagogic'. The ritual of representation has been preserved to a certain extent, with elections and councils, assemblies and the Congress all continuing to function. Powers of decision in the most important matters have, however, been completely usurped by the executive which itself is safely out of reach of popular elections.

Nor, moreover, should due attention fail to be paid to the shortcomings of the electoral system, which are the result as much of an inauthentic party political set-up, whether elitist or populist, as of authoritarian measures which prevent the electorate from demonstrating its will. However imperfect the electoral system has been at different periods of Brazilian political history, it was never as bad as it has been in recent years. To give an example in the case of São Paulo, it is enough to point to the contrast between the municipal council of colonial times, which both deliberated and governed, and the council of today, which neither deliberates nor governs.

The most important period in the political history of São Paulo did not really involve either of these extremes. Client-based politics was the leading feature of a lengthy process whereby ordinary people were brought into the political arena under the control of the economically dominant classes. As the concept of citizenship evolved, albeit in an abstract way, seen as independent of the individual's economic situation, it became necessary for political power to be legitimised by the people as a whole. Even though this did not in fact mean direct power for the majority, the holding of elections did influence the course taken by the government, if for no better reason that its need to win support among the people. Client-based politics functioned through the offer of personal advantages to the elector or, as was more often the case, governmental benefits to groups or sectors of the population in exchange for electoral support. In its most rudimentary form, it made the election of local councillors dependent on their ability to channel the benefits of local authority projects and amenities towards certain sectors of the population. This ability was sometimes exercised through making proposals or trading support in the council itself, and at other times by bargaining electoral support with the mayor or majority party. Local councillors were not so much representatives of the people as delegates for different interest groups such as professional, ethnic, religious or local bodies. In times of municipal autonomy, when the mayor himself depended on this kind of support to be elected, a balance was struck between the interests of the groups electorally most powerful in both the council and the Municipal Authority. In times when municipal autonomy was suppressed and the mayor was nominated by the governor, the influence of local councillors on the administration depended on their power to facilitate or hinder the executive's action, whether by legislative measures or by their ability to mobilise political support. In all cases, the political equilibrium in the municipality was temporary, since it had to be renegotiated at every election. By its very nature the manipulation of the vote under the clientele system made continuation in power dependent on the degree to which the wishes of electorally powerful groups were satisfied.

The incorporation of the people into the political process was more intense in São Paulo under the protective cloak of populism. Although the populist approach by no means excluded client-based vote manipulation but on the contrary made ample use of it, the greater mobilisation of the people under such populist leaders as Getúlio Vargas, Ademar de Barros and Jânio Quadros took place in a context of more general aspirations than those of individual electors and interest groups. Populism did not question the political and economic system which engendered such contrasting standards of living for different sectors of the population. It grew, however, out of a range of differing and opposed interests as a form of representation of less privileged sectors, allowing greater popular pressure to be brought to bear on the holders of political power.

A look at electoral results in São Paulo from 1945 to 1975 shows a reasonable degree of coherence in the way people voted.[61] The social bases of the political parties and populist leaders seem to correlate with the varying socio-economic conditions of the population. The currents of political opinion as expressed through the ballot-box reflect the division of the population by income and occupation, and the range of interests born of industrialisation and urbanisation.

61. See Simão A., 'O voto operário em São Paulo', *Revista Brasileira de Estudos Politicos* (1), 1956; Ferreira O.S., 'Comportamento eleitoral em São Paulo', *Revista Brasileira de Estudos Politicos* (8), 1960; Ferreira O.S., 'A Crise de poder do 'sistema' e as eleições paulistas de 1962', *Revista Brasileira de Estudos Politicos* (16), 1964; Weffort F.C., 'Raízes sociais do populismo em São Paulo', *Revista Civilização Brasileira* (2), 1965; Lamounier B., 'Comportamento eleitoral em São Paulo: Passado e Presente', in Lamounier B. and Cardoso F.H. (eds.), *Os partidos e as eleições no Brasil,* Rio de Janeiro, Paz e Terra, 1975.

Table 26, which draws on the results of a survey carried out during the 1974 elections, shows the distribution of preferences between the two parties in the city of São Paulo, for men and women of different social conditions. It shows that the preference for the Brazilian Democratic Movement (MDB)[62] among less-skilled workers is considerably greater than among businessmen, top civil servants, property-owners and people who do not work, while the reverse is true in the case of the Alliance for National Renewal (ARENA). The same tendency is apparent in voting according to districts. The MDB candidate for the Senate gained 70% of votes in the Capital while 19% went to the ARENA candidate and 11% were spoiled or left blank. These differences were not, however, randomly distributed in the municipality. In the 'non-working-class' residential districts of the centre-south region of the city, voting was in the proportion of less than 2 to 1 for the MDB. This proportion rises in predominantly working-class districts and as one moves from the centre towards the periphery. In the newest peripheral districts, which run from the north-east to the south-east of the city, at least 8 times as many votes were cast for the MDB as for the ARENA candidate. The proportions were less in the case of elections for the Chamber of Deputies. Even so, it is quite evident that the geographical pattern of voting follows the socio-economic divisions among the electorate.[63]

A question was asked in the same survey concerning the image of the parties, and the replies suggested that 'the parties have clearly identifiable features in the eyes of the electorate.' The most frequent reply from ARENA supporters was to the effect that the victory of their candidates would benefit all without distinction. As many as 60% replied in these terms, while only 8.8% said it would be 'the poor' or 'the working class' who would benefit. Responses from MDB supporters are in the completely opposite direction, for 31.5% replied in terms of 'the people as a whole', and 36.1% foresaw some advantage for the poor or the working classes. Since 'the nation' or 'the people in general' are extremely tempting constituencies for the self-image of any party, we have clear confirmation of the much referred-to predominance of MDB's image as the party of the less privileged.

62. Translator's note: MDB, *Movimento Democrático Brasileiro* (Brazilian Democratic Movement), is the official opposition party, while ARENA, *Aliança Renovadora Nacional* (Alliance for National Renewal), is the official government party. The two parties were set up by the military régime in 1965 to replace the parties in existence before the 1964 coup, which were at that time banned. The 1974 elections were partial national elections for the Senate and Chamber of Deputies.

63. See the maps of voting patterns published by Lamounier B., *op.cit.*, pp.23 and 25.

TABLE 26 CHOICE OF PARTY,
BY SEX AND OCCUPATIONAL STATUS
(IN PERCENTAGES)

Occupational status	Men				Women			
	ARENA	MDB	None	(Number)	ARENA	MDB	None	(Number)
Low-status occupations	14.9	85.1	—	(18)	13.1	72.0	15.0	(46)
Middle-status occupations	21.3	61.5	17.2	(136)	21.4	61.6	17.0	(85)
High-status occupations	27.6	48.9	23.5	(61)	27.9	48.6	23.5	(69)
Do not work	29.5	50.0	20.5	(65)	29.6	50.1	20.3	(360)
(number)	(75)	(148)	(57)	(280)	(148)	(307)	(105)	(560)

Observations:

a. Choice of party was measured by the question: "Do you prefer (or identify more with) either of the present parties: ARENA or MDB?"

b. Status was measured using an occupational strata classification, under which low-status occupations include paid domestic service, street sellers and odd-job men, semi-skilled manual workers and similar occupations. Middle-status occupations include skilled workers and poorly-qualified non-manual workers. High-status occupations include skilled-non-manual employment, managers and administrators, property-owners, etc.

c. 90 responses not classified under one or more of the three variables were excluded. The absolute numbers in the 'Numbers' columns and row are the *uncorrected frequencies*. The percentages however are based on the corrected numbers.

Source: Lamounier B., *op.cit.*

"Among those who, although supporting candidates, did not profess to be in favour of either of the two parties, the pattern of replies is particularly suggestive of the way in which the political system is seen by those who do not identify with any party. To begin with, the replies are very varied, most (34.9%) coming within the category of 'don't know'. Secondly, there is a notable increase in replies in the two categories which for the ARENA and MDB supporters are of little importance: 'politicians always act to their own advantage, or to the advantage of the government' (5%), and those who believe that no-one will benefit and 'everything will stay the same' (8%). Lack of interest and rejection of the political process, or at least a profound disappointment of expectations, are therefore the most likely attitudes associated with not supporting a party; while on the other hand, the ARENA and MDB assume distinct identities in the eyes of their supporters, the former as a party unattached to any particular group or class, the latter deliberately heedful of the interests of the less privileged".[64]

Surveys on electoral behaviour in the city of São Paulo reveal some degree of correlation between voting, socio-economic conditions and electors' aspirations. This does not imply that at any time the parties and candidates have necessarily behaved in accordance with their mandate as representatives of the interests and hopes expressed by those who voted for them. Nor does it signify that the voters all show the same degree of confidence in the parties and candidates they helped to elect. Nevertheless, the election results represent a symbolic expression of interests, varying in accordance with the social structure.

On the other hand, participation in voting does not mean that the city's population is participating in politics or in the political parties. Political parties in São Paulo have almost always restricted their activities to mobilising their leaders, candidates and electoral agents on the eve of elections. Only parties with more expressly ideological positions, whether of the left or right, and with a small number of active members have tended to carry out political work among the people outside election periods. Legal restrictions on overt forms of mobilisation, particularly on left wing organisations, have in turn contributed to limiting political activity to election times.

The results of the elections do not show that the interests of the different sectors of the population are represented by the party system. They indicate no more than a choice by electors between the various options open to them, within a system in which they do not participate. Moreover, a considerable proportion of the electorate has always refused to identify with any of the available choices. Table 28 shows the results in the state of São Paulo of the last three elections for the Chamber of Deputies. It can be seen that no less than 46% of voters, in 1966 and 1970, and 32% in 1974, either failed to vote, left their slips blank or spoilt their votes.

What the election results do indicate without any shadow of doubt is the profound dissatisfaction of the people of São Paulo with the political direction taken by the country. Despite the smallness of the vote received by the government party, changes have not been forthcoming in the rigidly-controlled political system.

It is unnecessary to stress again the symbolic nature of electoral activity when the possibility of power changing hands is known to be out of the question. It is, however, worth examining the reasons why the extent of

64. Lamounier B., *op.cit.*, pp.35-6.

opposition to the country's political direction, which becomes evident at election times, does not find equally forceful expression in autonomous social movements which question the whole political system. It is obvious that the same institutional framework which makes voting irrelevant also affects the possibilities of effective activity on other levels. The entire organisation of the Brazilian state is designed to prevent and, when necessary, repress organised forms of opposition. While legislation

TABLE 27 IMAGES ASSOCIATED WITH THE PARTIES,
BY PARTY OF THE INTERVIEWEE
(IN PERCENTAGES)

Images associated with the parties	ARENA	MDB	Neither
1. Will benefit the poor, workers, etc.	8.8	36.1	11.9
2. Will benefit the middle class	6.1	6.7	2.8
3. Will benefit the rich, the upper classes	3.9	0.6	1.0
4. Will benefit everyone, the nation in general	60.0	31.5	27.4
5, Will benefit the politicians, the government itself	0.2	1.8	5.0
6. Will benefit specified groups; mixed responses, responses not classifiable under the other categories	8.0	11.8	8.6
7. Will benefit nobody, nothing will change	4.3	2.2	8.0
8. Did not know; did not wish to reply	8.7	9.3	34.9
Total percentage	*100.0*	*100.0*	*100.0*
Number of responses	227	465	164

Source: Lamounier B., *op.cit.*

TABLE 28 RESULT OF ELECTIONS
TO THE CHAMBER OF DEPUTIES
(VOTING IN THE STATE OF SÃO PAULO)

	1966	1970	1974
ARENA	1,407,410	2,627,422	2,028,581
MDB	1,222,573	902,713	3,413,478
Blank and spoiled votes	1,449,828	1,870,763	1,675,809
Abstentions	821,683	1,147,937	906,731
Total	*4,901,494*	*6,548,835*	*8,024,599*

Source: Regional Electoral Tribunal.

forbids the organisation of political parties which oppose the regime, all political activity outside the framework of the official parties is repressed. Autonomous political movements, for example the mobilisation of students and workers in 1968, have only taken place in São Paulo when a crisis has rendered the means of repression ineffective; or when, as in the case of the armed left wing groups at the end of the 1960s and beginning of the 1970s, clandestine methods have been adopted. In both cases, the basic conditions were lacking for popular involvement in political activity in any permanent way, which gives meaning and content to social movements.

In a society in which citizens' organisations cannot express the variety of different interests and aspirations, politics becomes the specialised activity of politicians. Ordinary people are forbidden to concern themselves with questions of power, except when called upon to do so symbolically through the ballot-box.

Nevertheless, though electoral participation of citizens is, as a rule, symbolic, there are other levels at which they can express themselves more directly. As urban-dwellers and workers, their lives and their problems are undoubtedly determined by the general economic and political conditions pertaining in the country. If these general conditions do not escape their notice, as the election results indicate, why then should the immediate conditions which affect them as urban-dwellers and workers?

Organisations which represent the interests of certain sectors of the population both express the specific hopes of their members and at the same time reflect the general political and economic conditions in which these hopes have formed. The local associations in São Paulo are a good example of the relationship between specific struggles over local needs and general political conditions.

Local associations did not spring up merely from the knowledge that demands must be made if the deficiencies in urban living conditions are to be rectified. They are also the result of an awareness that, whether because of the rigidity of the political system or the municipality's loss of autonomy, the city's residents have no influence on the bodies set up to handle their problems. This in part explains the political weight which such organisations have had and the importance which movements for autonomy have assumed at certain times in the city's history. It also helps to explain the considerable mobilising power which local associations have shown at various times, although the proportion of the city's population which participates in them is only a little over 3%.

The associations known as the Friends of the District Societies sprang up in São Paulo in the post-war period of the resurgence of democracy and enjoyed a period of rapid growth during the 1950s. This was a time of intense political activity when both the parties and the populist leaders sought to win support. As far as is known, the first Friends of the District Societies originated principally from a simple change in the statutes of electoral committees immediately after the elections had been held. As far as the parties and political leaders were concerned, the new Societies could be used to keep their bases of support organised in the period up to the next election. For the residents of the areas most lacking in basic amenities, an organisation centred on the political leaders provided them with access to the authorities and in certain cases enabled them to secure improvements in local facilities and services.

After their inception in the post-war period, the Friends of the District Societies entered a second phase, beginning in the 1950s and gathering force towards the end of that decade, which involved a reaction against the interference of 'politicians'. Local movements were formed in an attempt to create new organisations in some cases openly in favour of autonomy which were closer to the 'people'. The campaigns for the municipal independence of Osasco, which was successful, and Pirituba, which was not, have elements in common with other local movements, in their awareness that there is one São Paulo of the upper-class residential areas (the 'gardens'), and another of the 'periphery'. Complaints over the distribution of resources in the municipality were frequent in this period which continued into the first years of the 1960s. Nor was it merely a question of calling for limited measures on the part of the authorities. The local associations brought into question the politics and form of the organisation of municipal power themselves.

The wider discussion of the city's problems, which originated in the local organisations, initiated a new phase in the history of the Friends of the District Societies. They began to meet at a regional level and jointly with other societies in the different areas of the municipality. The Friends of the City Society exerted a certain influence on the approach taken by other associations at that time. This society had been set up in 1934 by a group of influential people to draw attention to the need for urban planning in São Paulo. Even so, strong resistance was offered by many local association leaders to the presence of the 'aristocratic' sectors of the Friends of the City Society in their movement.

The mistrust of organised politics, the authorities and representatives of the ruling classes, and the desire for autonomy which was evident in many local associations did not, however, prevent these movements from becoming absorbed to a great extent by the administration and by government politicians. Since their inception, the Friends of the District Societies had organised in their local areas around demands for public services and community facilities. Except in the case of successful movements for municipal autonomy, the criterion of successful action was the concession to their requests by the authorities. During periods of greater political freedom and competition for popular support, the question of whether the Friends of the District Societies could maintain some degree of independence rested on their bargaining power and the pressure they could bring to bear on the authorities. Even so, as the fate of many societies demonstrates, the more convenient course was often to become subordinate to the authorities or to influential political groups. However, once the freedom to demonstrate and organise at grassroots level was ended, as is now the case, the granting of demands has come to depend almost exclusively on the benevolence of the authorities.

On the other hand, municipal reorganisation involving the setting up of Regional Administrations in an attempt at decentralisation, cushions local demands by treating them as technical problems. The Friends of the District Societies always concentrated their efforts on obtaining basic urban improvements: piped water supply, a sewage system, street lighting, bus services, paved roads, schools, health centres, nurseries, hospitals and housing. That these problems assumed a political aspect in the early days of the societies' existence was due to the relationship between politics and the way the city was administered at that time.

In São Paulo, client-based politics and, in particular, populism, functioned on the basis of a municipal organisation bereft of overall planning. Intervention by the constituted authorities in the life of the city was limited to the supplementary function of solving the problems created by the increasing activities of private enterprises. Obviously the priority given to the resolution of these problems was dictated by the degree of political power in the areas concerned. The Friends of the District Societies, as grass roots organisations in the areas most lacking in basic amenities, reflected the political weakness of the periphery-dwellers but at the same time represented the potential to build up that strength. Indeed, the very fact that these communities organised themselves introduced a new factor into the political balance in the city.

The local associations' loss of a political role in recent times does not show in 'apolitical' characteristics of their leaders. On the contrary, as is made clear by the declarations from their meetings, the local leaders see their activities as a form of political participation.[65] Moreover, the militancy of some local leaders in the political parties, mainly ARENA but to a lesser extent MDB, speaks for itself. The political weakness of the local movements is evidenced by other circumstances. Since, for instance, the real forum for decisions about local problems has been transferred from the municipal council to technical bodies and the government, well out of the hands of the electorate, the associations' ability to exert pressure disappears. The political militancy of the leaders of these associations does not show how politicised they are, but on the contrary serves to conceal their absence from the real power game. As in other situations involving the government party, ARENA-affiliated leaders of Friends of the District Societies are less representatives of the people to the authorities than representatives of the authorities to the people. Since it is impossible for them to influence the decisions which affect the community in which they live, they act as distributors of the government's largesse in those areas fortunate enough to receive it.

Table 29 shows the different kinds of activities undertaken by the Friends of the District Societies according to a survey carried out in 1970 by the São Paulo Municipal Authority. Although most continue to work for urban improvements and communal facilities, the proportion which devote themselves to recreational, religious and civic, welfare and educational activities is worth noting. These findings perhaps suggest that such activities are a substitute for the political and pressure group activities which

65. See particularly the 'Declaration of Principles' published in the *Anais do I Encontro das Sociedades de Amigos de Bairros da Grande São Paulo*, São Paulo, 1968.

TABLE 29 FRIENDS OF THE DISTRICT SOCIETIES:
RANGE OF ACTIVITIES
(IN NON-MUTUALLY EXCLUSIVE CATEGORIES)
SÃO PAULO 1970

Activities	% which carry on activity
Educational and cultural:	
MOBRAL basic literacy course	2.7
Regular school courses	6.7
Other literacy courses	6.7
Training courses	17.3
Supplementary courses	2.7
Clubs (for mothers, young people)	1.3
Cultural activities	5.3
Welfare	
Donations	41.3
Medical/dental assistance; help	
with acquiring medicines	12.0
Referrals	10.8
Assistance for minors, the family;	
legal assistance	8.0
Pressure group	
Urban improvements	88.0
Social facilities	65.3
Leisure and Sport	
Games	13.3
Outings	14.8
Parties	54.8
Religious and civic	24.0

Source: São Paulo Municipal Authority, Social Welfare Secretariat, Department of Social Integration, *Caracterização Tipológica de Entidades Sociais,* São Paulo, no date (*circa* 1972).

have been forbidden. Moreover, the relationship between the local authorities and the Friends of the District Societies suggests a mechanism of mutual legitimisation. The scope for bargaining between an unelected administration and local associations deprived of all power to exert pressure is restricted to the decision to recognise one another or not.

In spite of the various factors which have stripped the Friends of the

District Societies of their political nature as autonomous grassroots organisations, their role in bringing together certain groups and sectors of the population should not be overlooked. The kind of association they are currently beginning to form may prove a rallying point for those who are dispersed and disadvantaged by living conditions in the city. However, the loss of the original nature of the Friends of the District Societies together with the game of pressures and counter-pressures which formed part of it indicates the closing of a chapter in local politics.

The obvious result of the inability to exert political or electoral pressure on the tackling of city problems is the increased influence of the laws of the market in determining the contrasting standards of living. The votes of poor and rich are equal in the ballot-box. In a genuine contest, the majority could impose, if not a change in the rules of the economic game, at least a distribution of public resources somewhat different from the distribution of private income. However, given the inhabitants' impotence in deciding how their city is to be run, they are obliged to accept a form of urban organisation which simply reflects the income inequalities of the economic order.

The majority of the city's residents must either live as their low wages permit or obtain better wages. However, the usual method of advancing wage claims through the trade unions has also suffered from the general ban on political and social activity. Although the great majority of São Paulo's inhabitants are wage-earners and their families, only 15.74% of the population are members of trade unions.[66] On the periphery, where most of the working class live, the degree of participation in trade unions is even less, involving around 5% of the population in those areas.[67] Taking the occupational groups represented rather than the population as a whole, the number of union members in São Paulo is known to be between 10% and 15% of all the workers in the different categories.[68]

It is important not to confuse the numerical membership of trade unions with the degree of active support given by workers for mass meetings, campaigns and strikes. Moreover, the mobilisation of the workers in defence of their interests often goes beyond the organisational framework of the trade unions. The history of the workers' movement in São Paulo contains a number of examples of widespread mobilisation far exceeding the bounds of trade union membership. The general strikes in the Capital in 1917, 1953, and 1957, and in Osasco in 1968 are prime examples. However, particularly

66. Berlinck M.T., *A Vida como ela é*, Campinas, 1973.
67. CEBRAP, *Recursos Humanos da Grande São Paulo*, São Paulo, 1971, 2 vols.
68. This estimate is based on a comparison of the statistics for union membership with those for occupation.

during periods of greater civil liberties when the very frequency of workers' actions detracted somewhat from their impact, it has been clear that the involvement of workers in trade union activities expands at times of struggle, whether political or in pursuit of wage claims, waning once more with the return to the routine of welfare, leisure and cultural activities.

The low level of trade union membership in the country's largest industrial centre is explained not so much by local conditions as by the overall institutional framework which affects both the freedom of association and the right to express opinions and interests. Legal restrictions and political obstacles to workers' movements are so great that the trade unions tend to lose their members.

The presence of the state's guiding hand is not a recent phenomenon in the history of trade unions. Following the 1930 Revolution, the practices relating to labour relations were gradually brought under the control of federal law. The Consolidated Labour Laws of 1943 established the framework which remains essentially unaltered for trade union organisation. The trend since then has been to defuse conflicts between employees and employers by removing them from the workplace to specialised state bodies. Both organisation at work and coordination between the different sectors of labour have been impeded. The trade unions have been allocated the functions of representing workers before the Labour Courts and ensuring that the law is complied with, in addition to providing welfare and leisure activities. Political activity within the trade union has been banned. Finally, a number of measures guarantee the government's control of the trade unions: the imposition of a standard statute; obligatory recognition by the Ministry of Labour; strict control of trade union funds; intervention by the Ministry of Labour in trade union elections and the power to dismiss elected officials and replace them with government nominees.

At certain times in the past trade unions have been able to operate relatively independently of the government, a situation made possible by the balance of political forces which allowed them to function 'in spite of the law', ie. exceeding the legal limits placed on their activities without encountering any effective opposition. On the other hand, the governments which wanted to reduce the trade unions' effectiveness as representatives of the wage-earning classes have all implemented the same methods: enforcing strict compliance with the 1943 Labour Laws, supported by varying doses of coercion applied by the bodies in charge of state security.

Apart from their ever-present control over the trade unions' ability to pursue their demands, various governments have always tried to make political capital out of them, whether for electoral purposes or in an attempt

to win popular support. The corruption of trade union leaders has been a much-used weapon both by employers and by populist governments. The problem with *pelegos*[69] is that they tend to lose credibility and hence their validity as representatives, thus becoming useless for the purpose of manipulating the body of workers. The government has therefore often been obliged to recognise the real leaders of the workers' movement, negotiate with them and make concessions to them. Political mobilisation round the trade unions and the negotiating and bargaining which accompanies it have been stopped by post-1964 governments. This emasculation of the trade unions can partly be explained in terms of ideology: the fear aroused by conflict, negotiations and pressure which are common to all political activities also applies in the case of trade unions; concern over order, discipline and harmony is directed particularly at the area of production. In this way, the very concept of the role of the trade unions has come to be redefined. In the words of a former Minister of Labour: "The union must, then, make of itself a true service to all its members. Let it be a school, clinic, cooperative and club, so that it may deserve the name of the home of the worker and of the businessman, serving the family of the one and of the other, and it will perform its role as an instrument of social justice within the community".[70] Thus the trade unions' function is defined — instead of action groups, they are to be welfare-providers, complementing the work of the Social Welfare Ministry.

Ideological reasons, however, do not sufficiently explain so radical and unprecedented a redefinition of an institution which, since the time of the Industrial Revolution, has been known throughout the world as the workers' specific means of exerting pressure for better pay and better working conditions. Government policy towards the trade unions over the last decade only becomes fully intelligible and coherent in the light of its importance for maintaining a particular pattern of capitalist growth which tends to make wage-earning workers discontented. The move to reduce workers' incomes, vital for the success of the 'economic model', necessarily involved changing the framework within which trade unions operate. On the one hand, the fixing of wage levels could not be left to the vagaries of free collective bargaining. On the other hand, it was imperative to ensure that the principal sufferers, the workers, could not by their protests obstruct

69. Translators note: *Pelego,* meaning literally a sheepskin saddle, is the name given to union leaders in the hands of the employers or the government.
70. Barata J., *O Sindicato como Instrumento de Justiça Social,* inaugural lecture given at the Curitiba Law Faculty on 5 March 1970. (Translator's note: The 'businessman' is mentioned since unions exist for both the 'employing' and the 'labouring' classes.)

the onward march of production. It was therefore urged that trade unions be deprived of their specific role of collective wage-bargaining and their more general function as a channel for expressing the interests and opposition of the working classes.

One result of the new wage policy was the trade unions' loss of any influence in deciding the workers' level of pay. Extensive legislation, in particular law no. 4725 passed in 1965, stipulated that the percentage by which wages were to be adjusted,[71] which had previously been decided between the employers and the relevant trade union with the mediation of the Labour Courts, would instead be established for all sectors by the government, by means of a complicated calculation involving wage coefficients (decreed each month by the President of the Republic), inflationary residual (estimated by the National Monetary Council), and the average rate of growth of national productivity (decided by the Ministry of Planning). Furthermore it was decreed that the regional offices of the Ministry of Labour would not approve "collective labour contracts containing clauses or conditions specifying wage adjustments diverging from the established norms" (decree no. 57,637, of 13 January 1966). The concession of any increase or adjustment was also forbidden, even when granted as a result of job reclassification, until a year had passed since the previous agreement or negotiations over wages and working conditions (decree law no. 25, of 29 July 1966). Finally, any agreement was declared null if it contravened the standards of the government's economic policy as regards wage policy (article 623 of the Consolidated Labour Laws, as drawn up in accordance with decree law no. 229, of 28 February 1967).

Excluded from the process of deciding wage adjustments, trade unions were also deprived of an important weapon in their independent struggle against employers: the right to strike. The consequence of law no. 4330 of 1 June, 1964 was that the right to strike, guaranteed under the 1946 Constitution, suffered so many restrictions that it virtually disappeared from the armoury of legal weapons available to the workers. Strikes were forbidden for those in basic services: water supply, energy, sewage, communications, transport, freight loading and unloading, funeral services, hospitals and maternity clinics, basic foodstuffs, chemists, hotels and other essential industries as defined by the government. Strikes for political, religious or social reasons, or in support of or solidarity with other strikes are also banned. Strikes aimed at changing the conditions laid down in agreements or collective labour conventions or binding decisions of the

71. Translator's note: The aim of the new wage policy, in theory at least, was to 'adjust', not raise, wages, so that they would retain their real value in a high-inflation economy.

Labour Courts were also outlawed, as were those in pursuit of claims considered invalid by the Labour Courts and those which did not respect the legally-established dispute procedures, and waiting periods. These were deliberately designed effectively to preclude the right to strike. In effect, the only kind of strike permitted by law is that following the non-payment of wages by the firm.

In addition to their exclusion from negotiations, and being circumscribed in their ability to exercise collective pressure by means of halting production, the trade unions are also subject to increased control by the government. Of the different ways laid down in the Consolidated Labour Laws for disciplining the unions, ministerial intervention to remove elected leaders is perhaps the most effective and shattering. Moreover it has been used without restraint. Between 1964 and 1970, 536 interventions of this kind took place throughout the country. Of this number, 432 (or 80.6%) occurred in 1964 and 1965 and the reason given for 81.9% of these interventions was subversion. Interventions in the different sectors of the economy between 1964 and 1970 were as follows: industry: 49.1%; commerce: 11.3%; inland transport: 5.5%; education and culture: 1.7%; commerce and advertising: 3.2%; credit institutions: 8.6%; agriculture: 5.6%.[72]

Tables 30 and 31 give a more detailed picture of the extent to which this disciplinary measure was used. In the period 1964-5, there were in Brazil 2,049 local trade unions, 107 regional federations and 6 national confederations, which means that 18.7%, 42.0% and 66.7% of trade unions at the respective levels suffered ministerial intervention. In the state of São Paulo, 115 local trade unions, including the overwhelming majority of those in the Capital, and 7 of the 18 federations, were the victims of intervention.[73]

In the same way, between 1964 and 1969, 108 union leaders and political representatives of the workers were punished by the suspension of their political rights and/or had their election mandates annulled: 63 in 1964, 21 in 1965, 13 in 1967, and 11 in 1969.[74] These radical measures were complemented by legal amendments controlling the choice of union leaders. Foremost among these was item IV of article 530 of the Consolidated Labour Laws (drafted in accordance with decree law no. 229, of 28 February 1969), which banned from election to union posts "those who, openly and

72. Figueiredo M.A., *Política governamental e funções sindicais*, Master's thesis, draft text (mimeo), 1975, pp.31-57.
73. *Ibid.*, p.45.
74. *Ibid.*

TABLE 30 BRAZIL
INTERVENTION IN TRADE UNION BODIES
1964/65 AND 1966/70

Type of body	1964/65 %	(Number)	1966/70 %	(Number)	*Total* %	*(Number)*
Local union	79.3	(383)	20.7	(100)	*100.0*	*(483)*
Federation	91.8	(45)	8.2	(4)	*100.0*	*(49)*
Confederation	100.0	(4)	0.0	(0)	*100.0*	*(4)*

Source: Figueiredo M.A., *op.cit.*, p.43.

TABLE 31 BRAZIL
INTERVENTION IN TRADE UNION BODIES
BY REGION, 1964/65

Region	Unions Intervened	Total number of unions	% of interventions
South East	225	876	25.6
South	38	508	7.5
North East	102	492	20.7
North	7	91	7.7
Centre West	19	67	28.3

Source: Figueiredo M.A., *op.cit.*, p.49.

publicly, by word or deed, defend the ideological principles of a political party which has been struck off the legal register, or of an association or body of any nature, the activities of which have been ruled to be contrary to the national interest". Though less rigid than the 'certificate of political acceptability' created under the Dutra government (1946-51), this kind of regulation is sufficient for the ministerial authorities to ban a particular candidate or list of candidates whenever it suits their convenience.

On the other hand, a series of activities not very clearly regulated by law — holding of public meetings, the trade union press, the existence of groups within the trade unions opposed to the leadership, drafting of documents to the authorities, in short, the whole range of activities which make up the daily round of an independent organisation — have fallen into the vast area of uncertainty where the limits of legality are not known in advance, but decided, in each case, by the police authorities.

While the above account shows that the great majority of interventions in trade unions and reprisals against elected officials were carried out in 1964 and 1965, it cannot be inferred that the degree of vigilance to which the trade unions are subjected has been relaxed in recent years. Having purged the union leadership elected before 1964, the authorities have retained the power to intervene as the ultimate deterrent. To this extent, it is at the same time a threat and a reinforcement, guaranteeing that trade union activities are restricted to the permitted areas, ie. providing welfare services and checking on the fulfilment of social legislation by companies. However, reality does not always conform to expectations and obstacles have emerged to impede even the satisfactory performance of these two functions.

Even accepting the highly debatable definition of a trade union as a welfare organisation, the obvious question is its ability to benefit the majority of the workers it represents. In practice, though the funds raised by the trade union tax[75] are sufficient to allow trade unions to maintain themselves without voluntary contributions from those they represent, they would be in very short supply if the welfare services were to be used by all workers in the relevant occupational category. For example, if all the metalworkers in São Paulo were to join their union, the services it provides would collapse. Thus the welfare function imposed on trade unions places a ceiling on the number of its members, above which additional affiliations threaten the union's ability to continue operating. Obviously, the low rate of unionisation does not only result from the obstacles raised by the trade union's welfare role. It is the restrictions imposed on pursuing claims which are principally responsible for the lack of interest and the withdrawal of large sectors of the working class from the trade unions. Thus the trade union's function as an 'instrument of social justice' — in the official understanding of the term — is laughable, given the fact that it benefits only a small minority. Moreover, it contributes towards weakening the trade unions and rendering them unrepresentative.

The problems arising from the supervision of the application of social legislation are different. During the 1940s, in order to cushion class conflicts and to prevent a head-on clash between workers and employers, the state decreed a number of workers' rights concerning working conditions, thus obliging firms to concede to their employees by law what would otherwise only have been won by direct pressure. In this way, the Consolidated

75. The trade union contribution (or 'tax') consists of a compulsory annual levy corresponding to one day's wages for all workers, whether union members or not, which goes to finance the activities of the local union and federation of the occupational category involved.

Labour Laws established the nature and the scope of labour contracts (section IV, chapters I to X); standardised the definition of occupations and the registration of employees; regulated the length of the working day and conditions of hygiene and safety at work, dealing with such details as lighting, ventilation, personal hygiene, sanitation, canteens and drinking water, cleaning of the work-place and waste disposal; established the right to holidays and the proportion of foreign workers which could be employed, and regulated the work of women and children. This set of legal measures sought to deal with common problems likely to arise in the industry of those times, which was dominated by medium-sized firms. The function of each trade union which was only organised outside the work-place, was to ensure that this legislation was respected and, in cases where it was not, to bring a complaint before the Labour Courts. This watchdog function has remained a prerogative of the trade unions. However, profound changes in the structure of Brazilian industry have created new problems which were unforeseen in the legislation regulating working conditions and consequently procedures for their solution do not exist. These changes began to take place at the end of the 1950s when the large modern company, usually foreign-owned, began to play an increasing role in the country's economic development. Large-scale modern industry in São Paulo has generated new demands by its employees in areas such as productivity bonuses, recruitment, work rates, the system of classification and promotion, and so on. These new problems created by working conditions, themselves the result of the process of capitalist development, have revived the debate on trade union freedom, and on the very nature and function of trade unions in the present day.

In the first place, for many trade unions it is no longer enough to concern themselves with the implementation of existing legislation, though this continues an important duty. It is also necessary to win new rights. The struggle for new rights always involves processes of clarification, debate, meetings and mobilisation of the workers which require a degree of freedom of activity which trade unions are far from possessing. In the second place, problems arising in large firms and directly related to internal organisation are unlikely to be solved outside the work-place. On the contrary, they demand negotiations between the firm and its employees and hence some form of organisation of the workers. In other words, the operation of the trade union inside the factory is necessary, something which until now has neither existed nor been permitted. Nor is it enough that this organisation should exist and be recognised. It must also have the autonomy to negotiate freely and directly with management over the specific problems of those it represents. A trade union controlled by the state and existing only outside the work-place can scarcely perform this function effectively.

How have the trade unions reacted to government policy and to the new challenges posed by the process of development? Though excluded from wage bargaining, controlled and reduced to organisations providing welfare and legal services, the strongest trade unions in São Paulo have never in principle conformed to the role that has been thrust upon them. They have not become transformed into health centres, schools or clubs. Despite their restricted membership, they have still retained something of true trade unionism, which among other things has permitted the existence, under threat but nevertheless still there, of opposition groups in almost all trade unions. Though they have not been able to prevent the erosion of the workers' standard of living, their platform has continued to include denunciations of the wage-squeeze policy and demands for it to be revoked. Though they have not been able to oppose the multiple controls imposed by the Ministry of Labour and the daily surveillance of the security forces, they have not ceased to defend the principle of trade union independence and freedom from state control. Refusing to be transformed into mere welfare and leisure societies, a number of trade unions of workers in large-scale industry have managed to draft a list of new claims, including a call for free contracts between firms and employees through collective agreements; recognition of the right of trade unions to organise at work; wage increases in line with the growth of productivity. To summarise, even though the state has managed to dominate trade unions in São Paulo and impose its own system of economic growth to the detriment of the workers' standard of living, it has not been able to win their support and adherence. Like many other organisations which exist to advance the interests of sectors of society smothered by the ever-present state, trade unions in São Paulo have not died but gone into hibernation.

The inability of both trade unions and local associations to win demands is due to the same reasons which have reduced the channels of political participation to parties with little ability to win a following and whose occasional victories do not help to realise the fundamental aspirations of the workers. The limited possibilities of achieving basic rights under the established political system is reinforced by the minority participation in voluntary organisations geared towards action — which in principle should serve as channels for basic socio-economic demands.

This low level of participation does not mean, however, that such associations are not capable of playing an important role at certain times. Nor does it mean, on the other hand, that under certain conditions,

TABLE 32 PARTICIPATION IN VOLUNTARY ASSOCIATIONS
(AS PERCENTAGE OF POPULATION)

Voluntary association	São Paulo*	Periphery of São Paulo**
Trade unions	15.74	4.9
Professional groups	9.60	
Work-clubs	5.09	
District associations	3.12	3.1
Religious associations	2.66	8.4
Sports clubs	19.68	16.7

Sources: *Berlinck M.T., Hogan D., *Associações Voluntárias, Canal de Comunicação de Massa, Informação e Adaptação urbana entre as Classes populares na Cidade de São Paulo*, São Paulo, 1971, p.13 (mimeo).
**Cultura e Participação na cidade de São Paulo*, São Paulo, CEBRAP, 1973 (Cadernos CEBRAP no.14).

significant social movements cannot occur. Such movements have occurred in the past and there is no reason to assume that Brazilian society is in itself apathetic and devoid of initiative. However, the various initiatives which have taken place have been systematically controlled and contained. Hence, both the voluntary associations which have been based on concrete demands have lost effectiveness and autonomy, thus discouraging participation, and moreover, participation itself, when not restricted to the ritualistic and purely formal, tends to contain an element of danger which is often too much for potential members.

Despite the overall institutional framework which prevents individuals from joining action-oriented organisations, participation in such groups varies in accordance with people's economic level: in the case of six kinds of association in the city of São Paulo (trade unions, professional groups, local associations, religious associations, works clubs and sports clubs), 41% of the richest category did not belong to any. Of the medium income group, 57% did not belong to any, a figure which rises to 79% for the low income group.[76]

Looking only at action-oriented organisations, it is also evident that the degree of participation decreases as income level falls, except in the case of local associations, where it is low for all sectors.

A large proportion of the population, deprived of effective formal channels through which to press their demands, tackle day-to-day problems

76. Berlinck M.T., *A Vida como ela é, op.cit.*, p.191.

TABLE 33   MEMBERSHIP OF VOLUNTARY ASSOCIATIONS
ACCORDING TO SOCIAL STRATA
(IN PERCENTAGES)

Action-oriented groups

Social strata	District association		Professional group		Trade union	
	Member	Non-member	Member	Non-member	Member	Non-member
High	2.3	97.7	52.3	47.7	22.1	77.9
Middle	2.3	97.7	11.0	89.0	20.5	79.5
Low Middle	5.0	95.0	1.7	98.3	17.5	82.5
Low	3.6	96.4		100.0	2.5	97.5

Source: Berlinck M.T., *A Vida como ela e, op.cit.*, p.189.

through means which their personal relationships make available. The friends-and-relations network, however, presents a very narrow range of benefits, consisting of solutions of an isolated and individual nature rather than a collective permanent nature. Nevertheless, in the absence of practical possibilities for social participation, relations based on friendship, compaternity and common birthplace assume importance in the solution of everyday problems. (In Brazil, particularly among the working classes, there are close relationships between a godfather and the child's parents. The godfather or compadre is almost a relative.)

A study of low-income migrants showed that, on arrival in the Capital, half of them solve their problem of finding somewhere to live through family ties and 16% through friends.[77] When they encounter problems in relation to work, they seek a solution through their family, friends, or migrants from the same place of origin (40%), or through colleagues at work (29%); only 5% resort to the official channels. When the difficulties are financial, the same method predominates: only 6% use the official means. Even when the problem is one of health, 24% opt for informal solutions.

Personal ties are widely used by those sectors with no official channels to

77.   Godinho M.T., *Metropolização e Planejamento Social*, São Paulo, PUC, 1974, 2 vols. Study based on 540 interviews, carried out in November and December 1973 with people not born in the municipality, who arrived in São Paulo aged 14 years or more. The sample covered a group whose income, in 80% of cases, did not reach 3 minimum wages.

Religious and leisure associations

Social strata	Religious		Work-club		Sports club	
	Member	Non-member	Member	Non-member	Member	Non-member
High	3.1	96.9	6.9	93.1	63.9	36.1
Middle	3.7	96.3	8.5	91.5	35.1	64.9
Low Middle	2.5	97.5	4.7	95.3	8.8	91.2
Low	1.8	98.2	2.5	97.5	1.1	98.9

attend to their needs. Instead they seek to solve their problems through self-help. This is a common practice among periphery-dwellers, where exchanges of favours of all kinds exist among neighbours, friends and relations.[78] Help in building a house is common.[79] This can also be observed in the shanty-town when a relative or friend from one's home town arrives: the new arrival is given accommodation, helped to find work, lent money and given help to build a shack. Obviously this kind of assistance exists in all social classes. It is the poorest groups, however, which have most need of a self-help network precisely because they are least likely to join action-oriented groups and have least access to the resources provided by society.

In the event of unemployment, accident, illness, enforced removal or eviction, they resort to personal contacts. Trade unions, banks, organisations and associations are ineffective or involve complicated procedures. More than mere labour power is necessary to gain access to public resources. You have to provide guarantees, sign undertakings,

78. *Aspirações com Relação aos Problemas de Educação de Base*, São Paulo, SEBES, 1970 (mimeo).
79. Relatives, neighbours and friends have the following influence in the location of people's houses: 41.7% for the top-income group; 57.2% for the high middle-income group: 64.1⁰ for the low middle-income group, and 52% for the poorest group. But 39% of the latter build their own house, while the better-off groups buy theirs through an estate agent in 22% and 14% of cases: Berlinck M.T., *A Vida como ela é, op.cit.*, p.204.

TABLE 34 ACCESS TO INFORMATION
AND KNOWLEDGE OF SOME URBAN SERVICES
(IN PERCENTAGES)

Sectors	Communications media			Services not known			
	Does not see TV	Does not hear radio	Does not read newspaper	Major public hospital	Health post	Voters' registration office	Where to obtain identity card
High	1.5	3.8	2.3	2.3	4.5	1.5	—
Middle	2.1	6.9	8.3	2.6	6.6	5.7	2.3
Low Middle	5.8	11.8	32.4	6.4	8.8	16.1	8.0
Low	11.0	28.2	73.9	19.6	19.6	56.2	29.2

Source: Berlinck M.T., *A Vida como ela e*, *op.cit.*, pp.195 and 207.

possess documents, offer certificates of good conduct. To have rights, in other words, it is also necessary to have resources of one's own: knowledge, a skill, influence, property. To get prescriptions, medicines, a place at school, certain jobs and certain kinds of help, it is often necessary to obtain a recommendation, request or introduction. There are time-consuming bureaucratic procedures involving a variety of forms, dossiers, routines and paperwork. As jobs and benefits are difficult to secure, you have to know 'Dr so-and-so'[80] or a local 'bigshot' to help in submitting requests. It is all part of the circle of favours and paternalistic practices which maintain the beneficiary in a position of dependence. The rules of the game of dependency are not revealed by the one who dispenses the favours. It is he who retains the monopoly of the service, which is made available in exchange for the acquiescent loyalty of whoever receives the benefit. The essence of the 'bigshot' network is to have a friend in a certain place so that a job or other benefit not otherwise obtainable can be obtained. But the worst aspect is that the system of favours reinforces the existing hierarchy, of domination over whoever is in the subordinate position.[81]

This kind of subordination constitutes only one among many ties which maintain the working class in a state of dependence. The lack of information

80. 'Dr' is the formal term of address for people with a certain level of professional qualification; but anybody who wants to be somebody and who is in a position to dispense favours naturally assumes this title. (Translator's note).
81. Silberstein P., Favela living, personal solution to larger problems,' *America Latina*, 12(3), July/September 1969.

and the misinformation in the mass media, the surveillance of action-oriented groups — trade unions, political parties, voluntary associations of various kinds — and the control to which people are subjected both at work and outside, not to mention the practice of repression itself, combine to form a wide-ranging and complex system designed to guarantee the order and security necessary for the 'proper' functioning of society.

With the control over collective means of pressing demands, individual methods have become common. This often means that wider interests are ignored. A study of low-income inhabitants showed that 35% are not interested in problems affecting their daily lives. 20% of the remainder offer criticisms or solutions, while the other 80% read about, concern themselves with or discuss the problems, but always with the attitude of observers, perhaps because they know that the 'costs' involved in taking action are heavy and the results uncertain.[82]

Seeing little point in joining action-oriented groups and deprived of resources, the poorer sectors of the population also have less access to information from the mass media, especially the press, and are less knowledgeable about the various facilities which exist in the city. For considerable sectors of the population, participation in the city's life is limited to work and to the area where they live. Their main connection with what goes on in the world is television, around which many of them gather during the weekends and other free periods.[83]

More than half the workers who live on the periphery have a weekly day off work. They use this time to go visiting (20%), to go to the cinema (13%), or to football (9%), but the majority stay at home, watching live shows, the daily serials, or films on TV, or simply "not doing anything" (46%).[84] In this way, daily routine reinforces the isolation imposed by official restraints on communal association.

Controlled, contained, isolated, the inhabitants of São Paulo cannot expect any change in their way of life except through alterations in the institutional framework in which it exists. However, even though the political system prevents their effective participation in the usual forms of political and social association, there is no way of preventing their awareness of the problems they are up against and the obstacles which block their progress. Perhaps it is this very awareness which prompts the 'cunning' of everyday life and permits survival in the metropolis. Even the refusal of symbolic participation today could indicate that, when effective action does become possible, the moment will not be lost.

82. Godinho M.T., *op.cit.*   84. *Ibid.*
83. On the periphery of the Capital, 84% of inhabitants have a television set, and 75% claim to watch it regularly: *Aspirações com Relação ao Programa de Educação de Base, op.cit.*

Dictatorship and democracy

The facts and the analyses presented in the preceeding chapters offer a glimpse of the social and political environment created by the kind of development taking place in São Paulo. The economic exploitation and marginalisation of the majority of the people are accompanied and sustained by political control.

There are no lack of analyses demonstrating the 'mechanical', 'automatic', 'alienated' nature of people's behaviour in mass societies. It is easy to see how political apathy is reinforced by the fact that, in addition to the control of organisations and the expression of community interests, the ruling classes also manufacture a 'culture of illusion'. Technical progress in the field of mass communications, the fascination with television,[85] and the rigidity of the political system, are undoubtedly effective instruments to stultify, through enforced conformity, expectations which are always postponed to a vague future ("what I can't do, my children will do", "the future will be better than the present", etc.). The ideology of advertising ensures that consumerism — which for the majority does not even exist — is the supreme value of everyday life. Particularly noticeable is the illusion of consumerism amidst the reality of poverty, fostered through the widespread advertising of luxury items in such media as television, which reach those lacking even the essentials for survival.

---

85. "Each night, 7 million inhabitants of Greater São Paulo spend almost 3 hours in front of their television sets... Almost 95% of households in Greater São Paulo have a television. For Brazil as a whole, the figure is 50%". *O Estado de S. Paulo* newspaper, 14 March 1976.

However, it would be a mistake to imagine that the society of 'pseudo-abundance', created more by advertising than by mass consumption, has the magic power to impose acquiescence on every poor person who, bewildered and fascinated, watches commercials for the second family car. There is no reason to suppose that urban workers and people in general do not reinterpret the messages they receive. Reinterpreting, they refuse to accept images, fashions, values and beliefs which most profoundly contradict their own mores, values and possibilities of advancement.

Why should it be claimed that indoctrinating techniques and manipulation are bound to succeed in São Paulo? If this were true, every culture would be no more than the reflection of the dominant culture, and there would be no nook or cranny to harbour the work and the gesture which expose the deception and propose an alternative order.

If the perspective of an analysis is not limited merely to reinforcing the existing system, but aims instead to demonstrate the failures of that system in order to bring to light alternatives, the question arises of how to awaken the aspirations and interests of those who, deprived of their heritage, are continually subjected to the bombardment of a life-style and economic conditioning which seeks to reduce them to apathy and make them incapable of organising themselves.

Action to change the situation can be expected when it is realised that in imitating imposed standards, the behaviour of ordinary people is defensive rather than simply accommodating. Whenever Friends of the District Societies, a parish, a trade union, or even a political party (as happened in the November 1974 elections) proposes an alternative, *which does not endanger the survival and the basic interests of the person or the family involved in the protest,* a response occurs.

Some analysts, recognising the survival strategy underlying ordinary people's behaviour, have dismissed it as 'opportunist', or, from another angle, 'paternalistic'. Certainly a response is more likely to occur under the protective cloak of a recognised institution (church, political party, government) which provides a minimum guarantee of safety. However, the belief that apathy can only give way to opportunism or paternalism misses the point: the conformity of the masses is the result of a combination of the 'culture of illusion' and *repression.* The experience of poor people is not only one of economic and cultural deprivation but also one of the ruthlessness of the repressive machinery which exists in mass urban societies. It is no mere coincidence that one of the most deeply-felt sources of popular discontent concerns *security.* Security in this case should not necessarily be taken to mean the police. Often it means security against the abuses committed by the police, though it is not limited to this aspect.[86] It is this very concrete form of security — against arrest, against physical violence, against arbitrary dismissal from work — that the working classes seek to obtain through some recognised institution as a precondition for action. When they think that they can express themselves without fear of reprisals, instead of burning incense at the altar of advertising and consumerism, they give a resounding 'No!' to the predominant form of exploitation.

It is this need for security which often lies behind the search for religious experience as a refuge from the harshness and cruelty of society. São Paulo is witnessing the growth of various forms of popular religion: the influence of *umbanda*[87] and its magical vision of the world extends far beyond the ranks of its formal membership; the adherents of pentecostal sects represent at least 5% of the present population of São Paulo; and the growing popularity of certain aspects of the Catholic faith, such as the devotions to the saints held to be powerful protectors against the difficulties of this world, is to be seen in the pilgrimages to shrines and even in the number of thanksgivings to the saints put in the personal columns of newspapers.

From the so-called popular religions, whether the petitioning for intercession by saints, the acceptance of the strict ethic of the pentecostalists, or the devotions and rites of *umbanda*, emerge patterns of companionship and self-help which contrast with the pitiless rules to which São Paulo society is subjected. Though this deep popular religiosity may seem excessively pietistic, how can one not understand that, for the oppressed, the experience of salvation constitutes an escape from the more inhuman aspects of society? The importance which the different popular religions will assume in the future depends upon the direction of development of Brazilian society, in particular on the role of the churches and religious groups in the struggle to restore human dignity. Under present circumstances, the search for dignity is expressed through the experience of Christian salvation and the protective blessing of the *orixás* (*umbanda* deities).[88]

On another level, signs are emerging within the Catholic church of the superseding of conservative tradition as demonstrated by its activity in the

86. "A survey of public opinion carried out in October showed that out of every 10 people, no less than 7 live in fear of being arrested, against 6 in every 10 who are afraid of being assaulted": *Jornal da Tarde* newspaper, 12 November 1975, p.4.

87. Translator's note: An Afro-Brazilian religion involving magical rites and practices.

88. On religions in Brazil, see Camargo C.P.F. de (organiser), *Católicos, Protestantes e Espíritas*, Petrópolis, Editora Vozes, 1973; Fry P.H. and Howe G.N., 'Duas Respostas a Aflição: Umbanda e Pentacostalismo', *Debate e Crítica*, São Paulo (6), July 1975.

defence of human rights and of the moral values of Christianity. Particularly among workers, but also among young people and other social groups, the presence of the local church groups has provided not only new forms of social contact among the 'base communities', but one of the few channels of expressing the desire for justice.

In other church and religious groups similar signs of solidarity with the victims of oppression are emerging. How can religious participation which expresses the deepest needs of the oppressed be dismissed as 'paternalistic' or 'alienating'? How can people be censured for seeking whatever means of protection remain to them in an oppressive society to escape from their predicament?

The basic question is neither one of asserting the 'apathy' of the masses nor of condemning them for opportunistic conformity, but of recognising that, if the people are to organise themselves in the pursuit of their own interests, certain conditions are necessary. In other words, when it is accepted that the culture of the people is not simply a reflection of the dominant culture and that advertising techniques can only be fully effective when backed up by repression, the debate on the democratisation of society assumes a fundamental political importance. Moreover this debate becomes central once it is accepted that the model for a different society is not going to emerge by imposing the values of an 'enlightened' elite of whatever nature, whether a political party, a handful of heroes, reforming saints, or whatever, but from conscious, collective action, organised at the grass roots.

Democratisation in this context means the right of ordinary people publicly to express their points of view without fear of reprisals. On a number of occasions recently this kind of demonstration has taken place, thanks to the protection provided by recognised institutions such as the church and the political parties, which enabled popular aspirations to surface. Given the peculiarities of the situation in Brazil — in which traditional authoritarianism is now joined by technocratic authoritarianism — some form of protection is necessary if those who wish to express themselves are to do so without fear that the repressive violence of their rulers will be unleashed on them without appeal. From the people's point of view, though it may appear a purely negative and subjective definition, *freedom is the absence of fear.* By extension, a genuine democratisation will only be possible when channels are established at an institutional level through which people's feelings can be expressed without fear stifling their protest. The rule of law, although a necessary condition for this, is not in itself enough. It constitutes a necessary condition in that, by containing the violence of the state within legally-recognised limits and defining the bounds of its legitimate use, it makes possible the creation of other institutions through which people can act in safety. Through them and through their mediation, though not exclusively, a climate of confidence can be established which will allow what is theoretically guaranteed by law to become a reality: freedom from the fear of reprisals and confidence in the development of organisations and institutions capable of bringing people together and sustaining collective actions. The possibility of a sub-stantive democratisation also presumes a fluid communication system which will enable the exchange of experiences and desires, and the ability to propose practical alternatives (a process which itself requires consciousness-raising and education of the people) aimed at a more equitable social order able to guarantee employment, food and housing for all.

In other words, the ideology which promises consumption for the poor at some unspecified future date whilst in the present legitimising the wasteful luxury of the rich must be countered with the ideal of providing for the basic needs of the whole of society. Freedom and fear cannot coexist. Moreover there is no real chance of freedom whilst hunger, unemployment, lack of education for the children, and inadequate housing are cold shadows which darken the lives of the majority. In a society which accepts the scandal of average income differentials in the same firm of *100* to *1* (for this really is the difference, without any exaggeration, between executives and ordinary workers), it is necessary to counter by proposing more equal forms of pay. Furthermore, since inequality is based on the concentration of property, it is necessary to demand the *social use* of property (a principle written into Brazilian Constitutions), and a tax system capable of preventing abuse and avoidance, until a new social and economic order is found. It is as well not to forget nor to overlook the fact that (especially in São Paulo) not only rural property, but also urban property, is concentrated in a few hands, and urban property is perhaps the more important. Hence, without basic reforms in urban land use and in the tax system relating to inheritance and property, there is no way of reducing social inequality or, consequently, of providing for the basic needs of the majority.

Many other important questions also exist in defining the context in which the democratic movement in Brazil will take shape. The most important undoubtedly concerns the nature of the state and its relations with the social and economic order. The blocking of legal channels of popular representation and the impotence of civil society in the face of the authoritarianism of the state tend to encourage people to have recourse to personal relations and informal networks to solve daily problems. The organisation of various kinds of community associations at the grass roots could in this way play a decisive role in safeguarding individuals and allowing them to voice their most pressing needs. The general conditions for the restoration of human dignity and rights are outside the reach of these community associations. However, they could play an important part in helping to establish these general conditions, by acting as links, through the exchange of experiences and circulation of information, with a network of popular independent organisations.

The more general problems of the inhabitants of São Paulo, whilst they are problems which affect the inhabitants of the metropolis both as workers and as citizens, are not confined to the city limits. Hence, wider forms of organisation, both political and trade union, are essential instruments for the transformations which are so vitally necessary. Even though restrictions, whether legal or otherwise, exist on the free operation of popular organisations, the state is so far removed from social life that total control is impossible and there is always some room for legitimate action around the real objectives of the working population itself. These objectives are not necessarily the particular interests of sectors or groups of the population but imply above all alternatives to the existing organisation of society.

The provision of such basic human needs as work, food, education and a roof over one's head is essential for the establishment of genuine freedom. However, the struggle for these needs demands that currently available freedoms be used. These freedoms result from people's existing practices, which make use of the loopholes and the available channels and which encourage solidarity with one's fellows in order to form a common front against fear. From the people's point of view, freedom at present means bolstering the confidence of community groups and organisations in their activities. The path to a genuine democracy will lead through the formation and strengthening of numerous popular organisations. In this way, freedom will cease to be merely an unrealised legal principle and will instead become a way of life based on the provision of collective needs and on the respect for different beliefs.

These conclusions are incompatible with the idea that an egalitarian order can be imposed. Unless the different sectors of the people with all their different points of view participate through their organisations, any improvements in general living standards will be eroded by bureaucracy and elitism. The organisation of society to the real benefit of the workers can only be based on ample grass roots freedoms.

This book is the result of the condensation of various reports produced by the authors in 1975. The research was commissioned from CEBRAP — Centro Brasileiro de Análise e Planejamento, a private centre for research in social sciences — by the Pontifical Commission for Justice and Peace of the Archdiocese of São Paulo. Other research, simultaneously produced in CEBRAP by Bolivar Lamounier and Octávio Ianni have also been taken into consideration in the analysis. The research was co-ordinated by Lucio Kowarick and Vinícius Caldeira Brant. The translation includes some corrections of the original edition by the authors.